QUALITY OF WORK LIFE AND THE SUPERVISOR

Leonard A. Schlesinger
Harvard Business School

PRAEGER

PRAEGER SPECIAL STUDIES • PRAEGER SCIENTIFIC

Library of Congress Cataloging in Publication Data

Schlesinger, Leonard A.
    Quality of work life and the supervisor.

    Includes index.
    1. Personnel management. 2. Supervision of
employees. 3. Employees' representation in
management. 4. Job satisfaction I. Title.
HF5549.S242 1982   658.3'142   82-11291
ISBN 0-03-061598-4

For Phyllis, Rebecca, and Emily
who have given up so much for so long
with understanding, patience, and good humor

Published in 1982 by Praeger Publishers
CBS Educational and Professional Publishing
a Division of CBS Inc.
521 Fifth Avenue, New York, NY 10175 U.S.A.

© 1982 Praeger Publishers

23456789 052 987654321

Printed in the United States of America

Contents

Acknowledgments

The number of people to whom I owe thanks is considerable. Foremost among them are the managers, supervisors, and workers at the research sites described in this study, who provided the time, energy, and support for me to conduct my work.

During the study, I received financial support from the Harvard Business School Division of Research and the companies that cooperated in the research effort. Their support greatly aided me in completing the work in as uninterrupted a fashion as is physically possible.

My research and writing were greatly aided by Bob Le Duc of Hewlett-Packard and Arthur Turner of the Harvard Business School.

But most importantly I am grateful to Dick Walton, who has pushed me in this project from the beginning and who has influenced my entire thinking about organizations and quality of work life. Without his support, I might still be a first-line supervisor in a northeast Wisconsin paper mill.

1
Introduction

During the last decade we have witnessed increased interest in the implementation of workplace innovations designed to achieve significant improvements in employee productivity and quality of work life. These innovations in the workplace commonly address the ways in which rewards are distributed, in which workers relate to each other and to management, in which training is provided and career paths are conceived, in which information is channeled through the hierarchy, and in which responsibility is allocated for task accomplishment.

Virtually every one of these innovations has carried an implicit, if not explicit, intention to increase the level of participation in organizational affairs generally exercised by the shop-floor employee. This commitment to increased shop-floor employee participation appears to be rooted in a number of environmental characteristics and managerial beliefs: (1) increased education of entry-level workforce, (2) increased aspirations of workforce, (3) increased managerial concern for improvements in productivity in an effort to remain competitive in the international marketplace, and (4) a growing

1

belief that greater worker participation will lead to increased worker satisfaction and improved productivity.

The media have focused a great deal of attention in recent years on a limited number of highly visible workplace innovations, such as the work system designed for the start-up of a General Foods dog food plant in Topeka, Kansas, and the joint labor-management quality of work life project at the Bolivar, Tennessee, plant of Harman International Industries. Writers and researchers have analyzed and reanalyzed these limited data sets and have generally used the projects to confirm their personal beliefs and aspirations regarding worker alienation, blue collar blues, and the quality of work life. As a result, the conclusions the interested observer can draw from a review of the media accounts are often conflicting, and at best tentative.

At the same time, social science researchers have become increasingly involved in implementing workplace innovations and in measuring outcomes. A number of university and government-sponsored quality of work life institutes have been established, and a larger number of projects have recently gotten some attention in the business literature.[1] We are coming to a point where it is becoming reasonable to make some generalized assessments of the feasibility of a number of workplace innovations and to highlight the gaps in our knowledge that have created problems in many of the projects currently under way.

The primary concern of this study is to address a significant gap in our knowledge — an appropriate conceptualization of the first-line supervisory role in participative work systems. Virtually all reports of quality of work life projects recognize the supervisory role as a problematical one.[2] A wide variety of evidence is available to support this contention: Supervisors in participative work systems often express dissatisfaction with their role. They evidence high levels of ambiguity about their responsibilities and authority, complain that they lack either the skills or organizational support to do their job, and voice disappointment that they personally do not get recognition for the accomplishments of their subordinates commensurate with the effort they invest in their work. Typically they assume that they cannot get their own concerns attended to as readily as can most other groups in the organization.[3]

In the design of new organizations, management has not escaped the above difficulties. While one would expect to find problems in older plants when changing the supervisory role, one also finds such difficulties in new organizations, even among supervisors selected for their compatibility with management's conception of the role and acquainted with the organization's operating philosophy before accepting the job. In some cases the dissatisfaction expressed by supervisors in some of the new organizations has been evident to the point of difficulty in recruiting workers into supervisory positions.

Finally, confusion over the appropriate supervisory role is exhibited by the number and variety of titles and labels currently used by organizations to describe the position, for example, foreman, supervisor, team manager, team leader, coordinator, team advisor, resource person, and shift manager.

The intent of this book is to generate insight into the complex, dynamic role of the supervisor associated with increased levels of employee participation. In addition, it explores the responses of a number of different organizations to the problems raised by occupants of the supervisory role. The study proposes a conceptual framework for the supervisory role designed to assist practicing managers and consultants in their efforts to improve employee productivity and the quality of work life through increased employee participation.

QUALITY OF WORK LIFE

There are probably as many definitions of quality of work life as there are authors writing about it. Glaser[4] attempted to thread the various definitions into a coherent whole and outlined quality of work life activities as follows:

- Achieving sustained commitment from management to an open, nondefensive style of operations that includes sincerely inviting employees to speak up regarding problems or opportunities (a related element is provision of a practicable means for having members of the workforce participate in refining and implementing promising suggestions)
- Establishing a work environment that encourages continuous learning, training, and active interest regarding both the job and the product or service to which the job contributes (such an environment enables an employee to use and develop personal skills and knowledge,

which in turn affects involvement, self-esteem, and the challenge obtained from the work itself)
- Making the job itself more challenging by structuring it so that an individual (or work team) can self-manage and feel responsible for a significant, identifiable output if that kind of responsibility is desired
- Affording opportunities for continued growth, that is, opportunities to advance in organizational or career terms
- Training of supervisors to equip them to function effectively in a less directive, more collaborative style
- Breaking down the traditional status barriers between management and production or support personnel-achieving atmosphere of open communication and trust between management and the workforce
- Providing not only feedback with regard to results achieved and recognition for good results but also financial incentives, such as cost-savings sharing, where feasible
- Seeking to select personnel who can be motivated, under appropriate conditions, to "give a damn" about striving for excellence in task performance
- Evaluating and analyzing results, including failures, leading to revised efforts toward continual improvement

Few, if any, of the case studies reported represent the textbook application of each of the above activities. However, most of the cases we have researched have involved the introduction and application of a sizable majority of the activities. Each organization, of course, places different emphasis on these activities on the basis of environmental and other situational factors.

THE SUPERVISORY ROLE

What is the role of a supervisor in quality of work life projects? One thing is clear from a review of the literature: The role is not an easy one to fill.

Adizes[5] highlights the managerial role as having a dual focus, first as a leader:

> The manager must be self-confident. He should not need for the building of his inner security the power that a managerial position offers.

. . . He needs to be "other oriented" . . . must be willing to undertake the pressures that leaders experience when the followers do not instantaneously see the benefit of a proposal. . . . This style of leadership must be of the type that instills confidence that the manager is not only in control of the situation, but also that he expresses and implements the community's desires and aspirations. . . .

The manager must have the desire to develop the group, to improve group dynamics, to lead toward his own obsolescence. This he could do by constantly improving the managerial know-how of the group and by improving the channels and mechanisms of decision-making so that the group notes effective growth in its capabilities.

The manager will never develop the community to the stage where he will become dispensable. However, there must be some self-induced pressure to advance faster ahead in his own development than at the rate of growth in his group.

If it is not enough that this charismatic manager resolve the contradiction of controlling his or her own obsolescence while remaining better informed than those who will ultimately never be able to take over the position anyway, Adizes doubles the manager's burden by requiring that he or she be a traditional entrepreneur as well:

Entrepreneurship is the willingness to take risk vs. an identification and exploitation of opportunities. Leadership . . . is communicating this opportunity and its risks to the group and leading them to identify with the cause and the means suggested. . . . If the manager is entrepreneuring but not leading, the company might be advancing economically, but the group will not identify with the results and will view management as usurping powers and negating the group's sovereignty. . . . A leader who is not an entrepreneur might mobilize only to conservative relatively non-risk endeavors. . . . Pressure for conformity may bring about efforts dissimilar to the entrepreneur's original design. Since they can't identify with the product, they will leave.

Bernstein[6] outlines requirements for managers of worker-owned firms that are less elaborate (e.g., "must be able to balance workers' interests as wage earners and their interest as owners"), but his description of the traits required is equally complex and broad. Table 1.1 delineates the traits exhibited by power-holders, which tend to discourage or facilitate employee participation.

TABLE 1.1
Traits Required of Power-Holders (Managers)

Discourages or Prevents Employee Participation	*Fosters or Facilitates Employee Participation*
Desire to maintain exclusive prerogatives	Egalitarian values
Paternalism	Reciprocity
Belief that leader must set example by appearing infallible (tries to hide all mistakes)	Awareness of own fallibility, admits errors to workers
Governing from position of formal power	Governing by merit, explanation, and consent of governed
Mistrustful, believing that all others need close watching, hence intense supervision; limits freedom of subordinates	Confidence in others, hence willingness to listen and to delegate responsibility
Proclivity to secrecy, holding back information	Policy of educating workers, open access to information

Source: Adapted from Paul Bernstein, *Workplace Democratization* (Kent State University Press, 1976), p. 98.

Walton[7] recommends that applicants for leadership positions in participative work systems be carefully screened by exposing them to a set of "anxiety-provoking situations" created through role playing or other assessment center techniques.

Keysworth[8] speaks of the need for managers to demonstrate "a high level of technical excellence, . . . to support decisions with explainable logic since accountability will be total."

The sociotechnical literature, best exemplified by the work of Trist et al.,[9] talks about the role of management in quality of life activities as one of "managing the boundaries," of supplying groups with all the necessary information and tools for doing their job, and of managing the interface issues with other groups, the plant management, suppliers, and so on, so as to allow the group to go on about its tasks in a productive manner.

The set of expectations the above cited literature places upon managers in quality of life projects are for the most part broad and demanding. However, the realities of those who have been active in such work already raise some serious questions as to the relationship of these requirements to actual experience, as well as the capacity of these projects to provide an in-kind response to the needs of managers. It is those realities that this research addresses.

NOTES

1. For example, the American Center for Quality of Work Life (Washington, D.C.), the Michigan Quality of Work Life Center (Detroit, Michigan), the Work in America Institute (Scarsdale, New York), and the Center for Quality of Working Life at U.C.L.A. (Los Angeles, California).

2. Edward E. Lawler III, "The New Plant Revolution," *Organizational Dynamics* (Winter 1978).

3. R. E. Walton and L. Schlesinger, "Do Supervisors Thrive in Participative Work Systems?" *Organizational Dynamics* (Winter 1979), pp. 24-39.

4. Edward M. Glaser, *Productivity Gains through Worklife Improvements* (New York: The Psychological Corporation, 1976), pp. 3-4.

5. Ichak Adizes and L. Borgese, eds., *Self-Management: New Dimensions to Democracy* (Santa Barbara, California: Clis Press, 1975).

6. Paul Bernstein, *Workplace Democratization: Its Internal Dynamics* (Kent, Ohio: Kent State University, CARI, 1976).

7. R. E. Walton, "The Diffusion of New Work Structures: Explaining Why Success Didn't Take," *Organizational Dynamics* (Winter, 1975).

8. Stan Keysworth, "Worker Participation and Its Dividends for Management," *Personnel Management* (October 1975), 24-25.

9. E. L. Trist, C. W. Higgin, H. Murray, and A. B. Pollock, *Organizational Choice* (London: Tavistock, 1963).

2

Quality of Work Life and the Supervisor: A Conceptual Framework

This chapter presents the principal theoretical outcomes of the study in the form of a conceptual framework that describes, in general terms, the supervisory role under conditions of increasing self-direction in the work group.[1] This conceptual framework specifies a series of relationships among organizational, individual, and interpersonal variables, as well as supervisory satisfaction and effectiveness. The framework has been developed from iterative attempts at improving our preliminary model (outlined in the Appendix) at the conclusion of each site visit.

OVERVIEW OF THE MODEL: THE MAJOR CONCEPTUAL ELEMENTS

The model to be described in this study is comprised of six major elements:

1. Key tasks and technologies

2. Individual characteristics of human resources:
   Supervisors
   Workers
   Managers
3. Organizational design
4. Internal social system:
   Supervisor/work group relationship
   Supervisor/management relationship
   Supervisor/peer relationship
5. Organizational outcomes
6. Feedback and renewal systems

The purpose of this section is to define and briefly discuss each of the elements. Later sections focus on the ways in which the elements interact and lead to, or detract from, supervisor satisfaction and effectiveness.

Key Tasks and Technologies

The first, and central, element in our framework focuses on two highly interdependent factors: the key tasks of the organization (simply put, What is the organization in operation to create, and what are the steps involved in creation?) and its technologies (the major techniques, equipment, and so forth, used by the organization and its employees in carrying out its key tasks).

In considering the state of an organization's key tasks and technologies, one must address the following questions: What does the organization produce? What are the steps involved in the production process? Does it contain any key interdependencies? What is the organization's key technology? How complex is it, and what is the degree of labor and machine intensiveness? What demands do the key tasks and technologies place on the workforce in terms of such characteristics as (a) technical knowledge and capabilities; (b) information flows required; (c) physical effort required?

The answers to these questions vary dramatically; often, they differ significantly between two organizations that produce similar products.

Individual Characteristics of Human Resources

Organizations differ significantly in the makeup of the human resources they employ. Not only do they differ in number, with some firms employing 10 people, while others employ 250,000, but they often differ greatly in their individual characteristics. These differences are often attributable to locational aspects, which determine the labor force an organization has to draw on, but more often than not they represent an outgrowth of a conscious managerial strategy to recruit, select, and retain a workforce made up of a number of distinguishing characteristics.

For the purpose of our model, we must concern ourselves with the following individual characteristics of supervisors, workers, and managers:

1. Demographic data (age, sex, race, education)
2. Technical knowledge and capabilities
3. Previous work experience and its relevance to an employee's current position
4. Attitudes toward increased levels of worker participation
5. Desires for achievement, advancement, and promotion
6. Personal definitions of individual work roles

Organizational Design

By organizational design we mean the formal mechanisms explicitly designed to regulate the activities of an organization's workforce and equipment. These formal mechanisms include the recruitment, selection, socialization, development, and assignment systems for employees, the organizational structure (e.g., the design of jobs, departmentalization, the hierarchy and spans of control, rules), and the organization's operating systems (goal setting, planning, scheduling, measurement, evaluation, communications, rewards, and sanctions).

The precise nature of the formal mechanisms used by organizations varies significantly for a variety of reasons. In order to determine the state of a specific organization's design, we must ask the following questions:

1. What is the organization's formal structure? That is, what are the different departmental groupings and jobs? How is the hierarchy structured, and what are the roles, responsibilities, and levels of authority associated with each rung? What committees, teams, taskforces, and other groups have been set up to deal with specific issues, concerns, problems, or special projects?

2. What types of formal procedures are in place for establishing goals; planning and scheduling work flows; measuring and evaluating individual or unit performance; recruiting, selecting, socializing, developing, and assigning employees; rewarding and sanctioning employees; and communicating with employees?

Internal Social System

This element of our model is comprised of two distinct parts: culture and social structure. By culture, we mean those organizationally relevant norms and values shared by most employees. Social structure can be defined as the relationships among employees in terms of such variables as power, affiliation, and trust.

Whenever people are brought together into sustained interaction, a social system emerges. This system has a great deal of influence on the behavior of those people. For example, two hypothetical organizations identical except for their employees' norms regarding attendance will generate different behavioral patterns; the organization enjoying regular attendance norms will more likely experience less absenteeism. And so on.

As has been the case with each of the elements presented thus far, the internal social systems that evolve within organizations vary considerably. In order to determine the state of the social system in a specific situation, we must ask the following questions:

1. What norms exist among the three subgroups of employees (manager, supervisors, and workers) and influence their relationships with each other? For example, what norms, if any, exist among supervisors and workers regarding how closely workers are to be supervised, or what norms exist among managers and supervisors regarding managers' direct interaction with the workers?

2. What values exist among the three subgroups of employees? Do any of these values relate to what the organization should be or should achieve?

3. What types of relationships exist among managers and supervisors; supervisors and their peers; supervisors and workers/work groups, especially with regard to trust, levels of cooperation, and power?

Organizational Outcomes

The outcomes are what the organization actually produces both in terms of product and in terms of quality of work life developed within the organization. Outcomes are really end states that grow out of the organization's day-to-day activity reflected in the internal social system. Our measures of organizational outcomes go beyond a restricted focus on number of widgets per hour (even if that is all the organization has chosen to focus on) to a consideration of a broader measure of traditional business results, such as product quality, delivery, cost, labor efficiency, and turnover. However, we also move beyond the business outcomes to consider many of the outcomes that can be classified as being related to quality of work life, for example, improved opportunities for workers to use and develop their skills, greater worker influences over the decisions that affect them, increased self-esteem, and economic well-being.

For the purposes of this study, the focus is on such key organizational outcomes as supervisory job satisfaction and effectiveness.

Feedback and Renewal Systems

If we were to assess the state of the preceding five elements, we would have a picture of the organization at a specific point in time. However, a key assumption of this framework is that organizations are not static. We know that over time new technologies are introduced and that organizational designs change or other types of changes are introduced in an attempt to improve organizational outcomes. By feedback and renewal systems we mean the mechanisms that organizations create in order to collect information on the current state of the internal social system and organizational outcomes, evaluate the information, and change the organization if necessary, by influencing any of the other elements in the framework.

SUMMARY: OVERVIEW OF THE MODEL

The conceptual elements we have reviewed comprise an organizational model that we will use throughout this book to understand the supervisory role in participative work systems. An appreciation of all six elements is crucial to developing an understanding of the factors that influence both supervisory satisfaction and effectiveness, as well as organizational effectiveness.

This appreciation, when combined with an understanding of how these elements interact, will permit us to explain the phenomena observed at each of the field sites discussed in the case studies, as well as to make recommendations regarding action that will improve the lot of the supervisor in the participative work system.

We will now move to a discussion of how the six key elements interact to influence organizational outcomes. It will be useful to distinguish among three time frames, or stages in the life of an organization or plant: start-up (the first six to 18 months), shake-down (12 months to several years), and relative maturity (several years to decades). The discussion of stage 1 includes an examination of the dynamic interaction of the elements in the short run and focuses on the impact of such interactions on the supervisory role. Stage 2 is the shakedown period; the focus is on the fit among the six elements. Stage 3 applies to plants that are in a state of relative maturity; here, the focus is on the ability of the organization to maintain flexibility and adaptability in thinking about and acting out the supervisory role.

Stage 1: Plant Start-up

During a plant start-up, the most significant relationships among the elements in the framework are those that connect the key tasks with the organizational outcomes. In other words, the technology, individual characteristics, organizational design, and internal social system all provide the context for completing the organization's key tasks and achieving certain outcomes. (See Fig. 2.1.) At the same time, the feedback and renewal systems have an impact on each of the other elements in ways that help either maintain or change their state.

To clarify the dynamic relationships implicit in Figure 2.1, consider the following brief description of the first six months of operation of a plant offered by the plant manager:

In 1973 the demand for one of our new products rose to the point where our company authorized the construction of a new manufacturing plant. We designed the plant with a state of the art (and yet

FIGURE 2.1
A Framework for Understanding Organizational and Supervisory Outcomes

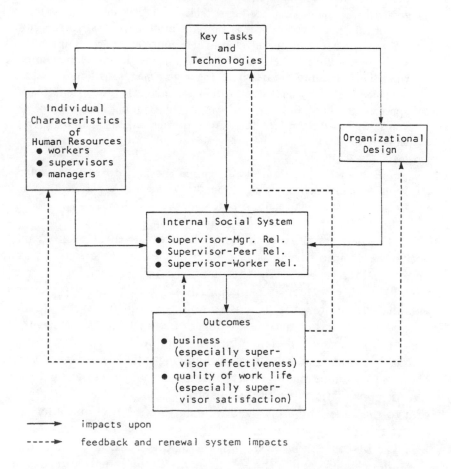

untested) technology in a location which had no other manufacturing facilities within a thirty mile radius. Therefore the employees we hired had little or no industrial experience.

The management of this plant was committed to running a plant where workers had the opportunity for significant and substantial participation in the day-to-day operation of the plant. We were so enthusiastic about the potential of employee participation that we were convinced we could start up the plant without any direct employee supervision whatsoever; we believed that employee loyalty and commitment to a successful operation would carry us.

Boy, were we wrong! It quickly became obvious (from looking at our results) that we had overestimated the ability of our workers to learn the production process and debug the new technology. Production levels were pitiful, quality was poor and our stock of worker goodwill was rapidly disappearing as their frustrations mounted. At the four month mark, we brought in upwards of 40 technical experts (on loan) to help us out technically and to help employees to get trained.

It was also clear that our notion of running without supervisors was either premature or infeasible. The management staff simply could not adequately stay in touch with our workers to the extent that appeared necessary. So we brought on board a contingent of six supervisors (we called them area advisers) to provide a tighter link between workers and management and to provide general assistance to operating teams.

Each of these actions assisted us in moving toward acceptable levels of performance within a month. Workers were pleased to get to a point where the operations were somewhat stabilized.

Within the framework shown in Figure 2.1, these events can be broken down into seven discrete inter-element interactions. In some of the actions reviewed by the plant manager, a structural element has some clear effect on organizational outcomes, for example, inability to master the new technology resulting in substandard production. In other actions, a key outcome triggers a response in one or more structural elements, for example, poor production and increasing worker frustration influencing management to secure technical assistance and to modify the hierarchy by adding supervisors.

An appreciation for the conceptual framework and its application to the time frame involved in a start-up requires an understanding of the two types of relationships presented in Figures 2.1 and 2.2. The first involves the shaping of the organizational outcomes by the other element, while the second involves the impact of those outcomes on the elements.

Shaping Supervisory Satisfaction and Effectiveness (Outcomes)

Examples of influence relationships going from the various elements to the outcomes are identified in Table 2.1. As one can readily determine, the range of sources of impact on the supervisory role is broad.

The key conclusion one should draw from this analysis is that the effect an element or a change in an element will have on supervisory

FIGURE 2.2
Start-up Relationships

1) A plant was designed with a new and untried technology

2) We were committed to high levels of employee participation

3) Our employees had little or no industrial experience

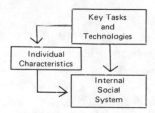

4) We started up with no direct employee supervision

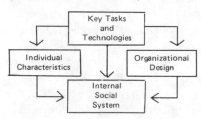

5) Production levels, quality, and worker satisfaction were all trending downward

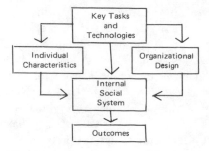

6) We brought in 40 technical experts on loan to help us out and to help employees get trained. We also brought on board a contingent of six supervisors

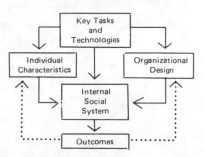

7) We moved to acceptable levels of performance within a month. Workers were pleased

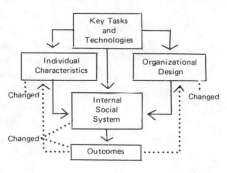

TABLE 2.1
Influence of Each of the Elements on Supervisory Satisfaction and Effectiveness

Element	Impact
Key tasks and technologies	The introduction of a new production technology completely changes the nature of the manufacturing process. Supervisors are ill equipped to master the technology or to lend assistance to workers who are having problems.
Individual characteristics	A group of recent MBA graduates have been added to a supervisory workforce consisting mostly of up-from-the-ranks non-college-educated people. The significant individual differences contribute to poor peer working relationships. Workers resent the new supervisors' superior attitudes.
Organizational design	A new worker appraisal system is introduced requiring the supervisor to file written evaluations of all employees on a quarterly basis. This practice is viewed as an extremely time-consuming assignment on top of an already heavy supervisory workload. Supervisors were not trained in appraisal skills, and workers are extremely dissatisfied with their sessions. A number of formerly positive working relationships deteriorate.
Internal social system	As a result of poor operating results during a workweek, management requests supervisors to spend the entire shift on the production floor and to closely supervise workers. Workers complain about supervisory encroachment, and supervisor-worker relationships deteriorate. Supervisors are angry with managers for making a unilateral request without consulting supervisors about potential alternative solutions.
Feedback and renewal systems	The mechanisms currently in place for feedback and renewal (or change) activities exclude supervisory input. While supervisors are expected to implement changes, they have little or no say in the analysis of problems.

satisfaction and effectiveness (outcomes) is a function of (1) the previous state of the organization's outcomes and that element and (2) the state of all the other elements. For example, at one research site, I was asked to comment on why the organization's worker appraisal program seemed to be ignored. In particular, the plant manager was concerned that a very carefully structured appraisal system (which represented a large investment of management energy) was not being adequately implemented. After a brief review of the situation, I found the appraisal system to be excellent. The problem was simply that the company's management did little or no performance evaluation either among themselves or with their supervisors and did not encourage their supervisors to keep their worker appraisals up to date. The impact of the managerial attitudes and behavior was much greater than that of the energy that went into developing the program.

The plant manager viewed the problem with a much more restricted focus, represented in Figure 2.3. On the basis of his model, the manager concluded that something was wrong with the appraisal system if it was not being used as it was designed. Our model enabled him to see that there was an alternative explanation to his problem.

On the basis of this new conclusion, the manager has recognized the need to focus on getting managers involved in conducting performance appraisals — beginning with himself.

The Impact of Outcomes on the Structural Elements

Examples of the ways in which outcomes can influence the other elements via feedback and renewal systems are presented in Table 2.2.

FIGURE 2.3
Plant Manager's View of the Problem

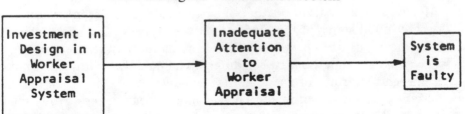

TABLE 2.2
Influence of Outcomes on the Other Elements

Element	Impact
Key tasks and technologies	Over time, the supervisory workforce has developed significant technical capacity, permitting the introduction of new complex technology into the operation with a minimum of problems.
Individual characteristics	Through the development of technical and administrative skills in the workforce, the composition of worker skills shifts considerably.
Organizational design	Significant achievements in business outcomes lead management to adopt a productivity gain-sharing plan for workers and supervisors.
Internal social system	As workers increasingly develop the capacity to regulate their own activities, the relationship with supervisors changes from a traditional boss-subordinate scheme to one in which the supervisor is more of a resource, advisor, or counselor.

Summary of the Start-up Stage

The key relationships in a plant start-up are between each of the elements and the organizational outcomes. Each of the elements shapes the outcomes; in turn, through the feedback and renewal systems, the outcomes have an impact on the elements in ways that help maintain or change their states.

In order to understand and predict supervisory satisfaction and effectiveness in a start-up situation, one needs to gather information on the initial states of the elements in the framework and to recognize the kinds of impacts that the elements have on outcomes, and vice versa. Key questions to be addressed include the following: What is the current state of each of the elements? What, if anything, is currently changing or might change in the near future? How will each change affect supervisory satisfaction and effectiveness (if it is a change in one of the elements), or how will a change in outcomes affect the elements?

Although helpful in understanding and predicting relationships during a plant start-up, this mode of analysis is too cumbersome and complex for the moderate (shakedown) and long-term (relative maturity) stages. If this model were applied, it would force the analysis of a countless number of changes and is simply impractical. As we move into our analysis of the shakedown period, we must examine the relationships that exist among each of the elements.

Stage 2: Shakedown

Over moderate time spans, organizations can clearly change a great deal. This change can adopt a wide variety of paths and often appears to be complex and incomprehensible. Our model permits us to understand the shakedown period by focusing on the relationships among each of the elements in the framework as well as the degree of their fit with each other. (See Fig. 2.4.)

Fit

Much of the research on organizational design and behavior conducted after World War II has focused on the relationships among two or more of the elements in the framework. The research concludes that when an organization's design, tasks and technologies, people, and social system fit together, one tends to find that positive outcomes are achieved.[2] If, however, the relationships among any of the elements do not fit, one tends to find less satisfactory results and an increased tendency toward organizational instability. By "fit" we are referring to a state of congruence or consistency among elements. Table 2.3 provides definitions of some of the more common fits.

The key role of the relationships among the elements in determining supervisory satisfaction and effectiveness during the shakedown period can best be viewed by examining a number of examples of misfits encountered at our research sites, reported below.

Individual Characteristics-Key Tasks and Technologies. The management of a two-year-old manufacturing plant had recently been confronted with a written list of concerns and complaints from their supervisors. The plant manufactured a limited number of products with a relatively simple technology. Its start-up workforce was relatively unskilled and required a great deal of assistance from the skilled

FIGURE 2.4
Relationships among Elements in the Framework

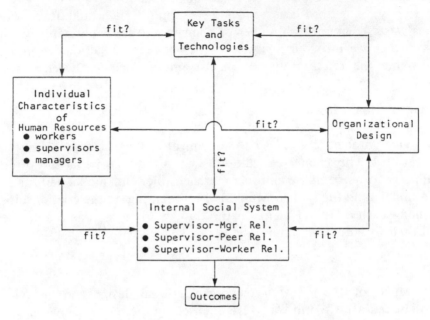

supervisors in learning the jobs at start-up. However, the employees rather quickly learned their jobs and achieved a sense of mastery over the production process, thereby lessening the need for the kinds of supervisory skills critical for a successful start-up.

Key Tasks and Technologies-Organizational Design. In this same manufacturing plant, the management group had designed a 52-month learning curve for training the average employee. Given the relative simplicity of the tasks and technology, employees were able to master them within 12 to 18 months. This error in the formal training system led to significant problems.

Organizational Design-Internal Social System. At all reported research sites, management had adopted a compensation policy that essentially rewarded what one knew rather than what one did. The various skills-based pay systems had met with varying degrees of success.

TABLE 2.3
Definitions of Fits

Fit	The Issues
Supervisor-organizational design	To what extent supervisors' needs are met by the organizational design; to what extent supervisors hold clear or distorted perceptions of organizational structures; the convergence of supervisors' and organizational goals
Supervisor-key tasks and technologies	To what extent the needs of supervisors are met by the tasks; to what extent supervisors have skills and abilities to meet task demands
Supervisor-internal social system	To what extent supervisors' needs are met by the internal social system; to what extent the internal social system makes use of supervisors' resources consistent with informal goals
Key tasks and technologies-organizational design	Whether the organizational design is adequate to meet the demands of the task; whether organizational design tends to motivate behavior consistent with task demands
Key tasks and technologies-internal social system	Whether the internal social system facilitates task performance; whether it hinders or promotes meeting the demands of the task
Organizational design-internal social systems	Whether the goals, rewards, and structures of the internal social system are consistent with those of the formal organization

Source: David A. Nadler and Michael L. Tushman, "A Model for Diagnosing Organizational Behavior: Applying a Congruence Perspective," in *Managing Organizations: Readings and Cases* (Boston: Little Brown, 1982), p. 43.

At two of the sites studied, supervisors and workers shared the responsibilities of determining when an employee merited a pay increase. The nature of the internal social system, which called for supervisors not to interfere in team affairs, led most supervisors to approve any increase approved by the team. This practice caused the two systems to be manipulated to the point where they became virtually seniority-based rather than skills-based programs. Major problems occurred when workers under regular production conditions needed to display a particular skill for which they were being compensated and were unable to carry out.

Key Tasks and Technologies-Internal Social System. As supervisors lowered their day-to-day profile with workers over time, the individual workers in one plant were expected to pick up the responsibility of communicating with departments with which they worked interdependently during the production process.

When such communications did not occur and problems arose, management would hold supervisors accountable for the often negative results. At the same time, any attempt on the part of the supervisor to become reinvolved in the interdepartmental communications process were met with complaints by workers of supervisory interference.

All the previous examples share a common pattern characteristic of the sites we studied during the shakedown. Something causes a change that creates a misfit among two or more of the elements in the framework. The task at each research site is to alter those states of misfit to recreate a relative fit. While the organizations attempt to solve the problems that result from misfits, they should maintain an awareness of the changes in other elements that are the source of further potential misfits.

The Supervisor/Worker-Work Group Relationship: Source of the Most Significant Misfits*

When managers design organizations that provide workers with an opportunity to assume additional responsibility and autonomy, they blur the distinction between what has traditionally been conceived as a supervisory role and a worker's role. Consider, for example, Dunnette's list of critical dimensions of effective leadership performance of the traditional supervisory role.[3]

1. *Know-how:* The supervisor keeps thoroughly informed of organizational needs and keeps up to date technically.

2. *Responsibility:* The supervisor is ready and able to accept personal responsibility for actions.

3. *Integrity:* The supervisor maintains high standards of business, professional, and social ethics.

4. *Wisdom:* The supervisor exhibits informed commitment and loyalty to organizational goals, policies, and practices.

---

*This section is adapted from Leonard A. Schlesinger and Richard E. Walton, "Supervisory Roles in Participative Work Systems," *Academy of Management Proceedings* (1978).

5. *Empathy:* The supervisor shows personal concern and under-standing for other persons.

6. *Communication:* The supervisor communicates effectively, thoroughly and accurately.

7. *Representation:* The supervisor presents a positive organiza-tional image to the public.

8. *Motivation:* The supervisor motivates subordinates and others through example and challenge.

9. *Training:* The supervisor determines subordinates' training needs and institutes programs to meet these needs.

10. *Coaching:* The supervisor provides direct performance feed-back to subordinates and shows them how to improve performance.

11. *Coordination:* The supervisor negotiates and cooperates with other organizational units for optimal use of all resources in meeting organizational goals.

12. *Innovation:* The supervisor develops and applies innovative procedures to accomplish organizational goals.

13. *Planning and allocation:* The supervisor forms goals and allocates resources to meet them.

14. *Delegation:* The supervisor assigns tasks to others and moni-tors performance.

15. *Accomplishment:* The supervisor persists with consistent high effort in all facets of performance.

16. *Crisis action:* The supervisor recognizes critical problems and acts promptly and decisively to alleviate them.

17. *Follow-up and documentation:* The supervisor documents actions and keeps accurate records of results obtained.

These 17 statements of what the supervisor ought to do are presumably valid and integral elements of Dunnette's ideal role defi-nition in a more conventionally organized work system.

Most of the participative work systems studied placed a cluster of additional oughts on the supervisor. In effect, the 17 elements of leadership ought to be relatively widely diffused throughout the work unit for which the supervisor is responsible. The supervisor ought to supervise in a way that enables workers to assume responsi-bility for most or all of the required coordination internal to the unit and some external to it, to train each other, to take on many of the planning functions of the unit, to problem-solve in crisis situations, to develop innovative procedures to improve on normal operations, and to coach each other and sanction counterproductive behavior of fellow workers. In other words, one might say that supervisors are expected to delegate as many of their functions as possible. A good supervisor is one who learns to work himself or herself right out of a job — at the same time grooming a set of successors. Thus, although delegation is an issue in any managerial position, it becomes both conceptually and practically the cornerstone dimension of the supervisory role — and ultimately of the organizational dynamics — in participative work systems.

Figure 2.5 presents a conceptualization of the supervisor/work group relationship that depicts the delegation of previously supervisory functions to workers and work groups, as their skills develop over time.

FIGURE 2.5
Conceptualization of the Supervisor/Work Group Relationship

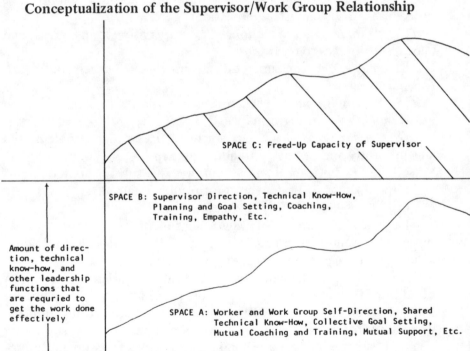

SPACE C: Freed-Up Capacity of Supervisor

SPACE B: Supervisor Direction, Technical Know-How, Planning and Goal Setting, Coaching, Training, Empathy, Etc.

Amount of direction, technical know-how, and other leadership functions that are requried to get the work done effectively

SPACE A: Worker and Work Group Self-Direction, Shared Technical Know-How, Collective Goal Setting, Mutual Coaching and Training, Mutual Support, Etc.

Time

Undeveloped Work Group ⟶ Relatively Developed Work Group

As Figure 2.5 indicates, at the outset, new workers and newly formed work groups are assumed to possess limited technical know-how and limited skills in organizing themselves to coordinate their efforts to make decisions and solve problems. Therefore, in order to fulfill the technical, administrative, and social requirements of the task addressed, supervision, or some other resource, must supply much of the expertise and play a largely directive, high-profile role. With time and appropriate training and development opportunities given to workers, the state of many of the elements shifts along with a corresponding shift in the load of day-to-day responsibilities. As workers and work groups develop the capacity to direct their own activities and to increase their technical capabilities (Fig. 2.5, space A), the supervisor's active role relative to the group and the task should tend to shrink in a directly corresponding pattern (space B), freeing up a capacity for supervisors to assume other functions (space C).

The sites studied have used this freed-up capacity in a number of ways — all based on being changes in organizational design and in the internal social system designed to bring about a fit between the two elements:

Enlarging the Supervisor's Span of Control. At the start-up of one plant, the plant manager announced the intention of eliminating the supervisory role in five years. At the three-year mark, each supervisor in the plant had a span of control averaging 50 employees. The span of control for supervisor at its sister plant was 15 employees.

Pulling Down Higher Managerial Functions. As one plant marked its first anniversary, supervisors were upset over the amount of dead time they were beginning to find themselves with. The plant manager encouraged them to meet as a team and to determine the functions currently performed by higher management that they would like to assume.

Pulling in Staff Specialist Functions. Supervisors at one plant were performing a number of formerly staff specialist functions. Some supervisors were actively involved in employee selection, some were performing quality auditing roles, and others were doing engineering design work.

Adding New Functions to the Supervisory Role. Two of the plants' management addressed the issue of freed-up capacity by adding a number of new functions to the role; for example, supervisors were expected to hold regular one-on-one meetings with each of their employees and to document each meeting as well as develop and implement equipment downtime reduction plans. Supervisors were also expected to participate in a number of meetings on different issues never before addressed by them.

Assigning the Supervisor to Short-Term Project Responsibilities. At many of the plants participating in this study, supervisors were routinely removed from supervisory roles to undertake such short-term project responsibilities as training program design, housekeeping, and plant upgrading.

A number of additional oughts for the organization can be readily derived from the foregoing conceptualization. For example, the organization must provide for investment in training to develop the technical and organizational skills required in order to make delegation a viable option. The organization must ensure that the supervisor has some net positive incentive to delegate functions to the work group. Moreover, the organization must consider how to employ productively the freed-up capacity of supervisors when they do successfully work themselves out of some of their supervisory jobs.

Analysis of Misfits among Key Elements

A number of common fallacies underlying the design and implementation of participative work systems have contributed to the misfits observed between the supervisor/work group relationships with other elements.

Neglect of Start-up vs. Shakedown vs. Relative Maturity Distinctions (Organizational Design-Individual Characteristics). In several instances, it was assumed that the work teams would start at an advanced state of development. Neglected was the important distinction between conceiving the design of the relatively mature organization and designing the start-up organization. Thus, the organizational design presented to newly hired workers and supervisors reflected that idealized for the relatively mature organization. In fact, workers initially lacked the technical and human skills, and their groups lacked the problem-solving capacity to be self-directing and to perform effectively. When it became clear that it was necessary to raise the profile and involvement of the first-line supervisor in teams that were floundering, the unrealistic expectations of team members had to be revised downward, thereby risking the cynicism of teams and complicating supervisors' efforts to gain legitimacy in exercising directive supervision.

The extent of the differences between start-up and relative maturity conditions, and therefore the length of time it takes to develop capacities of the workforce to handle large doses of delegation significantly, depends on the technical complexity of the production technology. An insufficient understanding of the production technology has led to problems in a number of the sites studied.

Unrealistic Assumptions Regarding Developmental Trends of the Work Group (Organizational Design-Internal Social System). Managers often operate as if there were an identifiable trend line on the self-direction learning curve that never plateaus or reverses itself — even in organizations in which work groups take time to develop. Consequently, organizations and supervisors are not prepared for the possibility of supervisors having to return in a higher profile role as a result of a dip in a group's capacity for self-direction. Our conceptualization in Figure 2.5, which depicts a possible development path of workers and work groups' capacity for self-direction, shows a few temporary setbacks in the maturation process. It can also plateau at a level below its peak. Many conditions can lower the level of development. For example, interpersonal conflicts or rival cliques can emerge, decreasing the ability of a group to reach consensus; an additional shift or unit can be started up, creating turnover, which will lower the level of technical skill in the initial work groups; and technological developments can occur that render workers and work groups temporarily or permanently more dependent on external direction and support.

Insufficient System Stability (Organizational Design-Internal Social System). Managers often pay inadequate attention to the need to provide for as much stability as possible in implementing innovative supervisory roles. For example, after adopting a self-managing team concept for workers who worked single shifts in a three-shift operation, supervisors in one plant continued to rotate shifts every six months. Six-month tours with a group did not permit the development of effective personal relations and mutual understanding regarding role responsibilities.

Underestimating the Need for Recruitment and Selection (Organizational Design-Individual Characteristics). In most instances, recruitment and selection of personnel for this dynamic supervisory role have received inadequate attention. In some instances, supervisors with no technical or managerial experience were hired to start up a plant with complex technology and inexperienced employees. These supervisors had very little to offer their work groups and during this early developmental phase were rapidly relegated to a "go-for" role. In other instances, plants hired highly experienced supervisors who could manage this early phase, but who lacked either the requisite attitudes or skills to let go of their functions and assist work groups in their development. In yet another situation, college-educated supervisors were brought into an organization for an initial assignment designed to last one to two years and were moved out when they had developed sufficient skills to make a contribution to their work group's development.

Underresourcing Supervisory Skills Development (Organizational Design-Individual Characteristics). Many projects observed, including some with a heavy training effort directed at workers and work groups, failed to recognize fully the need for new supervisory skills. As a result, inadequate training generally has been provided for supervisors who must deal with a highly participative work group. Furthermore, these organizations offer few role models for supervisors whose role it is to develop a subordinate group to the point where they are no longer needed. At higher levels of management, generally little attention has been paid to the importance of exploiting the informal coaching opportunities available in manager-supervisor interactions. Such developmental activities can provide supervisors with a model to guide their behavior vis-a-vis work teams.

Supervisory Evaluation and Reward Systems Not Tied to Team Development (Organizational Design-Task and Technology). Few of the workplace innovations studied have attempted to tie evaluation, measurement, and reward systems directly into the supervisors' mandate to reduce greatly their presence or to work themselves out of a job. Most managers and supervisors who participated in this study have not clearly outlined the extent to which they wish workers to participate in the management of their organizations. Consequently, developmental benchmarks around technical, administrative, and social skills are not built into the systems. In two organizations, an innovative mentality developed that tended to overemphasize the uniqueness of their particular organization and rejected the application of traditional managerial tools, such as evaluation measured against goals.

Absence of Supervisory Support Systems (Organizational Design-Internal Social System). Surprisingly many projects have been developed in a way that belies an early assumption that no provisions need be made for attending to supervisors' needs to share feelings with each other about this tension-laden role and to develop their own voice in the organization. In most projects the recognition comes after the need is felt most acutely. Efforts to build a team of those in interface roles have usually been well received. The underlying fallacy might be some notion that only the quality of work life of workers counts. The worst thing that can happen, and it has happened, is that supervisors, too, accept that underlying fallacy.

Summary of the Shakedown Stage

As the examples growing out of the supervisor-work group relationship point out, a variety of factors lead to misfits that are problematical for supervisors. The most common factors are related to the time span in which workers are developing skills to become effective contributors and participants to the organization and the structure created for supervisors to respond to and support the workers.

An understanding of the sources of potential and current misfits can assist managers in understanding and dealing with organizational problems. The following questions are helpful in diagnosing a supervisory system during a shakedown: Are any of the relationships among key tasks and technologies, individual characteristics, organizational design, and internal social system in a state of misfit? What types of changes appear to have created these misfits?

To this point we have outlined the usefulness of our framework in analyzing the start-up and shakedown phases of an organization. The knowledge we have gained regarding supervisory behavior and outcomes over the short and intermediate run do not provide us with the tools to analyze the supervisory issue over the long run in relatively mature organizations. That is the focus of the next section.

Stage 3: Relative Maturity

As plants grow older, the states of each of the elements tend to increase in complexity. New and different technologies are often employed. The individual characteristics of workers, supervisors, and managers tend to shift with the acquisition of new skills, the development of new attitudes, and the addition of new people. Additional organizational design features are incorporated to respond to new needs or to address existing problems. The ways in which the individual organizations in general, and the supervisory role in particular, evolve over time exhibit considerable diversity.

During the early stages of a plant's life, these elements generally are in easily identifiable states and, more often than not, are relatively easier to change than in later years. Over time, the states of these elements not only increase in complexity and diversity, but often gradually assume positions that are difficult to adapt. Our concern over the long term is to develop an awareness of the most significant or key factors and their areas of potential impact on outcomes and the ways in which they can be maintained in a state that promotes adaptability and flexibility.

Key Factors

In considering the impact of each of the elements in our framework on supervisory satisfaction and effectiveness (as the organizational outcome — the primary focus of our study), we must recognize that they are seldom equal. Often some elements are more influential than others and remain so for significant periods of time. For example, in high-technology environments, the key tasks and technologies element is often the most influential. In well-established (almost institutional) organizations, internal social system and organizational design are often the most significant elements. In many young organizations, individual characteristics of managers, supervisors, and workers often tend to be much more influential than are other elements. The same often holds for labor-intensive manufacturing organizations.

However, as outlined in Stage 2, there is generally a good deal of interdependence among each of the elements. If we find that one or two elements are clearly more significant than the others, we will identify these elements as key factors for the organization. The direction they move in often determines the way in which other elements change, in order to avoid creating a misfit among the elements.

Let us consider some examples from our field research that highlight the concept of key factors. One of the plants studied began operation in 1973, with the tasks and technologies and organizational design acting as key factors. The plant's manufacturing operations represented the technological state of the art, as did many of the parent company's other facilities. In addition, the management of this plant was transferred from other company operations. These managers brought with them many of the formal organizational design characteristics that were commonplace in the plants they were coming from. The prestart-up process was one of minor modifications of the older plants' organizational designs to fit the new plant's technology. The plant has been successful over the past five years by continuing to fine-tune its formal design and by continually upgrading the state of its available technology, with the other elements undergoing marginal adjustments to ensure a constant fit among the elements.

Another of our plants started up in 1975, with the internal social system as a key factor. The plant adopted an operating principle of "people helping people," a motto that was to guide all their efforts. The composition of the workforce, task definitions, and organizational design were all intended to support the operating principle. After a rocky start-up period, the plant has become quite successful. To date, all potential actions continue to be tested against the people-helping-people principle.

The concept of a key factor is not new. However, the notion that any of the elements can serve as a key factor is new. The bulk of the literature on organizational behavior argues for the external environment or for top management to serve as the key factors.[4] Our framework does not accept this notion. Although some elements serve as key factors in more situations than do others, any of the elements can maintain the capacity to serve as a key factor.

Providing for Flexibility

The discussion of stage 2 provided clear evidence that supervisory satisfaction and effectiveness over the long run lies, for the most part, in an organization's (and the supervisors') capacity to adapt to change. We can argue the logic of this conclusion as follows:

1. Each of the elements in our framework has the capacity, and often the tendency, to change over time. Because the elements are interdependent, a change in one element tends to exert an impact on one or more of the others. Therefore, a large number of changes in an organization are inevitable in the long run.

2. Changes in one or more elements can easily create misfits that can have a negative impact on supervisory satisfaction and effectiveness.

3. An organization's ability to correct misfits (i.e., to adapt) will directly affect supervisory satisfaction and effectiveness over the long run.

Research on organizational behavior concludes that an organization's ability to be flexible and to adapt to changes over the long run is largely a function of the state of its elements. Each element in our framework can range from extreme inflexibility and constraint to great flexibility and lack of constraint. The more constraining an element's state, the more difficult it is to change it over the short or long run. As numerous attempts at changing the state of the element encounter problems, the organization (and for purposes of this study, supervisors) will find itself increasingly unable to make necessary changes, and major problems will result. Table 2.4 presents a number of examples of element states that inhibit and promote flexibility as well as necessary adaptation in the supervisor's role and in organizational outcomes.

The more a plant's elements resemble those in the lefthand column, the more problems (in the supervisor's role and/or in the total organization) it will face in the long run, and the greater the chances that it will experience major difficulties in attempts to address them. The opposite is true for the righthand column. Without the regular application of time, effort, and resources, it becomes easy for each of the elements to move into states that inhibit flexibility. Much of the literature on organizational behavior focuses on the individual characteristics or the internal social system as the keys to maintaining a flexible organization. Although no doubt important, these elements by no means provide a total picture. An inflexible technology or organizational design has the capacity to inhibit organizational flexibility (or flexibility in the supervisory role as well).

TABLE 2.4
Key Elements and States That Inhibit and Promote Flexibility

Elements	States That Inhibit Flexibility	States That Promote Flexibility
Key tasks and technologies	The plant operates with a single complex technology that is becoming outdated and that requires substantial capital outlay for modification and/or replacement.	The plant operates with state-of-the-art technology along with a number of alternative technologies that serve as backups and/or models for the future.
Individual characteristics	The workforce is underskilled for the key tasks and technologies and possesses many skills/capacities that are not useful under the current mode of operation.	The workforce is highly skilled. There is some redundancy among skills, and employees possess some skills it might not need now but that might be useful in the future.
Organizational design	The organizational design is neither sophisticated nor complex, but is applied in great detail, uniformly across the organization.	The organization recognizes the need for and maintains different systems for structuring, measuring, rewarding, selecting, and developing people who perform different types of tasks.
Internal social system	Key relationships and norms are supportive of maintaining the status quo. Levels of trust and morale are low. Workers, supervisors, and managers have little sense of a shared purpose.	Key relationships and norms are supportive of flexibility. Levels of trust and morale are high. Workers, supervisors, and managers have a high degree of shared purpose.
Feedback and renewal systems	There is little collection of data relating to the current state of each of the elements and/or outcomes. Changes are implemented without recognition of the interdependence of the elements.	Formal systems are in place to monitor changes in outcomes and other elements and to change the organization accordingly.

35

Summary of the Relative Maturity Stage

We have argued that the key factors and the flexibility and adaptability of each of the elements in the relatively mature plant are the critical influencers of organizational outcomes. The key factors determine the direction in which the plant (and the supervisory role) evolve over time, and the states of the individual elements help determine the ability of the organization to be both flexible and adaptive.

The following questions are helpful in understanding and dealing with organizational issues over the long run: Does the organization have one or more key factors? If so, what are they? Why? In what direction is the key factor moving? What does that imply for the long run if the other elements change in order to avoid misfits? To what extent does each of the elements inhibit or promote flexibility? Is the organization investing resources to make the elements flexible?

However, the key factors and states of the individual elements do not necessarily help us understand the supervisory role during start-up or shakedown periods. For example, in a plant in which three or four of the elements are in states that inhibit flexibility, there will undoubtedly be difficulties in the supervisory role over the long run. By contrast, if the elements are in a state of fit, there will not necessarily be problems during the shakedown period, and if the elements are in states supportive of desired outcomes there will generally not be problems over the short run.

Summary of the Model

The framework outlined in this chapter recognizes the dynamic nature of organizations and of the supervisory role under conditions of increased employee participation. Table 2.5 provides an overview of the types of relationships and interactions among the elements that contribute to organizational outcomes — and to supervisory satisfaction and effectiveness.

Chapters 3-6 use the framework presented here to analyze the nature of the supervisory role at four research sites. The case studies are followed by a discussion of the implications of the findings both for managers and for further research.

TABLE 2.5
Stages and Characteristics of Plant Development

Time Frame	Major Relationships and Interactions
Start-up (6-18 months)	Direct relationships between individual elements and organizational outcomes, and vice versa
Shakedown (12 months to several years)	Relationships — fits or misfits — among the elements, in conjunction with start-up interactions
Relative maturity (several years to decades)	Key factors and flexibility of the elements, in conjunction with shakedown and start-up relationships and interactions

NOTES

1. Our conceptual framework draws on work done by John P. Kotter of the Harvard Business School and reported in *Organizational Dynamics* (Reading, Massachusetts: Addison-Wesley, 1978).

2. John P. Kotter, Leonard A. Schlesinger, and V. Sathe, *Organization* (Homewood, Illinois: Richard D. Irwin, 1979).

3. Marvin Dunnette, in *Man and Work in Society*, ed. E. L. Cass and F. Zimmer (New York: Van Nostrand-Reinhold, 1975).

4. Robert Miles, *Macro Organizational Behavior* (Santa Monica, California: Goodyear Publishing Co., 1979).

Case Study: Plant O

OVERVIEW OF THE PLANT

Plant O was one of 12 plants that comprised the Consumer Paper Products Division of the Century Corporation.* The plant was opened in 1969 by the XYZ Paper Company and operated for several years under XYZ management. A number of negative business factors forced XYZ to close the plant in the spring of 1973 and to sell the facilities and operating equipment to Century a few months later. Century retooled and redesigned the operation to meet its requirements and began operations in early 1975.

Plant O was located in a multicultural southwestern community with a large Hispanic population. Other minority groups were represented in the community, but not in any sizable numbers. The local economy was primarily agriculturally based, with high levels of

---

*All identifications relating to the plant and to the company have been disguised.

unemployment. The local lifestyle was characterized by high mobility and great attention to leisure-time activities.

At the time of this study (October 1977), the plant employed approximately 900 people distributed across a three-shift, seven-day operation.

INTEREST IN CREATING A PARTICIPATIVE WORK SYSTEM

The Century Corporation was a recognized U.S. leader in workplace innovations that promoted employee participation. In concert with the company's practices in this area, Plant O became the third plant in the Consumer Paper Products Division to enlist the assistance of internal and external behavioral science consultants to guide a group of approximately 60 managers, supervisors, and hourly employees through an open systems planning process intended to develop the organizational design for the facility. This group was comprised of ex-XYZ employees, managers from other Century facilities well versed in innovative organizational designs, and other managers from more traditionally run plants.

Management in the Consumer Paper Products Division attributed a good deal of the success of its newer facilities to the organizational designs that grew out of the open systems planning process and to the ownership of, and commitment to, the organization created and developed by the process. The same positive results were expected from Plant O.

KEY TASKS AND TECHNOLOGIES

The key tasks and technologies of Plant O can be divided into three distinct categories: papermaking, paper conversion into end products, and warehousing and shipping.

Papermaking

Plant O had one papermaking machine that was intended to supply all the needs of the paper-converting operation. Because the plant did not have its own pulp mill, it was dependent on local supplies, as well as on some of the pulp-making facilities of Century Corporation at other locations, for its raw materials supply. The papermaking process at Plant O, although it had a high degree of computer control, still required the art of experienced papermakers for efficient operation.

The paper machine was a highly complex piece of equipment requiring continuous maintenance and monitoring. If problems, such as a break in the paper being produced as it was being rolled on the cores, were not spotted quickly, major time losses on the machine could easily occur. The machine was operated on a three-shift, seven-day operation with occasional down days for scheduled maintenance. Each shift crew consisted of approximately seven hourly employees, a shift supervisor, and maintenance and electrical support personnel available in the plant on an as-needed basis. The process was obviously quite machine intensive.

Those employees involved in the papermaking operation generally possessed the most sophisticated technical skills of the production employees in the plant. Given that the plant was a vertically integrated production operation, all other production departments were totally dependent on the quality and quantity of papermaking production for their raw materials inputs.

Paper Conversion

Once the paper came off the paper machine, it either went into a work-in-process inventory or directly to one of two converting operations: toilet tissue or paper towels. With some minor variations, each of the converting operations was basically similar in process terms. They were responsible for rewinding paper into appropriate size rolls while embossing perforations that allow the end user to tear off sheets from a roll, cutting the rolls of paper into appropriate-size widths, bagging the product, and boxing the product into shipping cases.

The paper-conversion operations required significantly less sophisticated operator skill than did the papermaking process and were a great deal more labor intensive than papermaking. Some of the converting responsibilities could easily be learned in a few days. However, some of the tasks required a similar art on the part of an operator in order to get the most out of the operating equipment.

Toilet tissue was manufactured on a three-shift, seven-day basis, with approximately 30 people on each shift. Paper towels were manufactured on a two-shift, five-day basis, with approximately 25 people on each shift.

In both the papermaking and converting operations, many employees' jobs were reduced to a monitoring role when the operation ran smoothly.

Warehousing and Shipping

Once produced, the end product was moved to the warehouse to be stored until customer orders mandated its loading on a truck or railroad car for shipment. During the early days of Plant O operation, constant pressure was placed on the paper-converting operation to produce at a level to meet customer demand; often the product was being loaded for shipment directly from the production site. This pressure on converting was evidenced in the need for the converting operation to be extremely flexible in terms of running different products with rapid product changes and, in turn, translated into pressure on papermaking for higher-quality paper that would be easier to run on the converting equipment.

The warehousing and shipping tasks revolved around keeping inventory and other records and using forklift trucks to cart the work in process and finished goods inventories throughout the plant.

It is important to recognize the critical interdependencies that existed among the major tasks in the production process. Each was responsible for providing the basic inputs into the next process: papermaking to converting; converting to warehousing and shipping; and finally warehousing and shipping to the customer.

INDIVIDUAL CHARACTERISTICS OF HUMAN RESOURCES

Supervisors

At the supervisory level, the management of Plant O operated with a deliberate mix of ex-XYZ company supervisors, supervisors transferred from other Century locations to Plant O, and recent college graduates. Table 3.1 presents an overview of the makeup of the papermaking and converting supervisory groups.

Of the 11 manufacturing supervisors, all but two had a technical education or extensive industry background before assuming their current position. The rationale for the current composition of the supervisory force was stated by managers as follows. First, a decision was made to recruit a number of well-regarded XYZ supervisors to work in the facility under Century management. It was thought that these supervisors could provide both a valuable link to the XYZ workers hired to work in the plant as well as information of the suitability of XYZ workers for continued employment. They represented a base of in-depth understanding of the Plant O community and culture, information useful to the plant designers and start-up management. They also had a level of papermaking and converting expertise that would be difficult to duplicate without wholesale "raiding" of supervisors from other plants or engaging in an extremely costly and potentially risky process of trying to train a whole cadre of inexperienced paper industry supervisors to start up the plant.

Second, Century management had made a conscious decision a number of years earlier to strive for a deliberate mix in the composition of its supervisory force. Although precise percentages were never established, Century management had staffed itself with a core of technically proficient and experienced supervisors who would serve as a continuity force. It was generally recognized that most of these people would spend their entire career in a supervisory position. The rest of the supervisory force was filled from the college recruiting program, with people slated to begin their Century manufacturing management careers with on-shift supervisory assignments on tracks of one to three years. The rationale behind this assignment was that the skills and knowledge developed in the manufacturing supervisor's position were critical to success in other manufacturing management positions. While this notion was increasingly being called to question, and a number of new recruits were being started in other positions, it still represented the mainstream of management thinking and was acted upon accordingly.

Also, it was hoped that the skills and knowledge that continuity supervisors brought to the job (generally technical and process oriented in nature) would be transferred to new recruits through their interactions, while the engineering, administrative, and organizational skills possessed by college graduates would be shared in return. While this, in fact, occurred at times, it was not without a series of negative side effects that we shall explore later.

TABLE 3.1
Composition of Plant O Supervisory Force

Employee	Sex	Age	Years with Plant O	Years with Company	Previous Paper Company Experience (years)	College
				Papermaking		
1	M	23	½	½	None	B.S., Mechanical Engineering
2*	M	42	3	4	11 4 (supervisor)	None
3*	M	37	3	4	11 1 (supervisor)	None
4*	M	52	4	4	22 8 (supervisor)	None
5	M	29	2	2	None	B.S., Mechanical Engineering

				Converting		
1	M	35	1	2	None	B.S., Engineering Management
2	M	36	½	9	None	None
3	F	28	3	3	None	B.A., Psychology
4	F	32	1	6	None	B.S., Biochemistry
5*	M	45	3	3	13 1 (supervisor)	None
6	M	27	2	3½	None	B.S., Chemical Engineering

*Former employees of the XYZ Company.

45

Workers

The hiring practices and affirmative action goals of the plant (20 percent female and 30 percent minorities) reflected a management decision to have a workforce that adequately represented the Plant O community. All indications were that management succeeded in this area.

The description for the workforce that consistently came up in interviews was one of diversity. The workforce was characterized variously as competitive, family-oriented, and part of a working culture. There was a broad mix in the age distribution of the workforce as well as in educational background.

A large portion (approximately 40 percent) of the workforce consisted of ex-XYZ employees. These employees represented a valuable base of experienced personnel, many of whom had participated in the original plant start-up. As the community was primarily agriculturally based, there was no other pool of manufacturing-trained labor. This fact, combined with locally high unemployment rates, led to a widespread perception of Plant O as an attractive place to work.

Managers

The start-up management group, many of whom continued to work at Plant O during the study, was chosen for its previous successful experience in start-up situations. Many of the managers had previous experience in other Century participative plants and brought this additional unique expertise to bear on the Plant O design and organization. Virtually all the Plant O managers had, at one time in their career, held one or more supervisory assignments.

One unique aspect of the Plant O management group, given Century's promotion-from-within policy, was the hiring of the XYZ plant manager to run the Plant O facility under Century's ownership. His knowledge of the facility, the community, and the workforce was believed to warrant such a move.

The Plant O management group was most often characterized by themselves, as well as by supervisors and hourly employees, as high powered, hard chargers, and tough, people-oriented managers.

ORGANIZATIONAL DESIGN

Structure

All the Century Paper plants, with Plant O being no exception, operated under a matrix structure, with minor variations, as outlined in Figure 3.1.

At the head of this organization was a regional manufacturing manager who was responsible for the operations of three to five paper plants. Generally, they were headquartered at Century's main offices and visited plants on a regular basis (six to ten times a year) for performance reviews. Reporting to the regional manufacturing manager was the plant manager, who had ultimate day-to-day responsibility for plant operations. Each plant manager maintained a plant manager's work team composed of key reports. These reports were generally the unit operations managers, each of whom had responsibility for a number of manufacturing departments, the industrial relations manager, the plant industrial engineer, the plant engineer, and the plant chemical engineer. The plant manager's work team was generally viewed as a board of directors in the sense that they held oversight responsibilities for the health of the plant, policy development and implementation, managerial career planning and development, and various other issues. Each unit operations manager supervised two to four department managers. These department managers had oversight responsibilities for a single paper machine, for a number of final product-converting operations, or for the warehouse and shipping operations. A department manager along with the maintenance manager, industrial and chemical engineers, and the two to eight manufacturing supervisors comprised the department manager's work team. They met regularly to review operations, exchange information, plan future operations, and address problem areas.

Manufacturing supervisors were assigned to work teams ranging in size from six to 40 employees. They generally provided the only managerial presence in the plant outside daytime working hours and rotated work shifts along with their work teams.

Century practiced a relatively strict promote-from-within policy, hence, virtually all upper level managers had some direct manufacturing supervision experience.

FIGURE 3.1
Plant O Organization

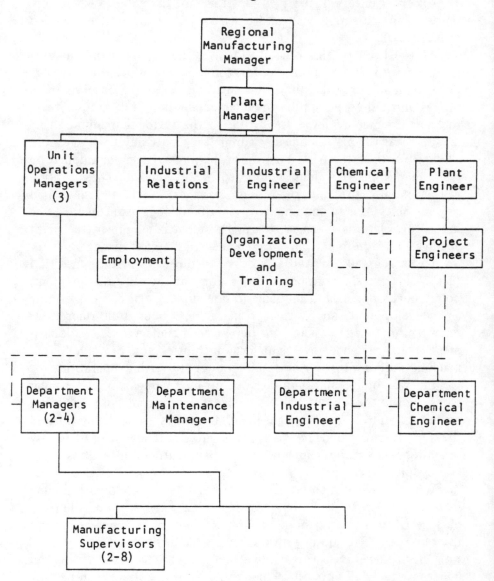

In addition to the direct manufacturing organization described above, a number of staff support services were available on site. Most unit operations managers supervised an industrial and chemical engineer, who maintained a dotted-line relationship to the plant industrial and chemical engineers. The plant engineers supervised a number of project engineers, who worked on area projects under the dotted-line supervision of a unit operations or department manager. And the industrial relations manager coordinated a staff of employment, training and development, organizational development, and industrial relations specialists.

Production requirements, product specifications, and marketing plans were generated at Century's headquarters and were implemented through consultation with each of the plants. The manufacturing plants viewed themselves as a true service function for the corporate marketing effort and were expected to respond appropriately to corporate requests.

Operating Mechanisms

Hourly Employee Pay and Progression System

On the basis of successful experiences with similar pay and progression systems at other Century plants, Plant O adopted a skills-based technician system that replaced traditional seniority-based notions with a system based on exhibited skills and competence. The rationale behind the pay and progression system was spelled out by the original design group as follows[1]:

> In designing the Plant O Pay and Progression System, we have made the assumption that the needs of the individual employee can be congruent with the company's needs through increased productivity. That would be achieved by improved results and reduced costs. An individual's progression in this system in developing skills would achieve this improvement in productivity. Our belief in this assumption is shown by the fact that the average wage rate in our plant has been pegged at a higher level than in the paper industry and that our pay rates are higher than comparable jobs in comparison industries.
>
> It is the intent of the Technician System to support the basic productive purpose of the plant. The system is not intended to be an end in itself. When we begin taking action to satisfy the technician system itself, we are violating the basic intent.

Progression in the system was achieved through the acquisition of knowledge and skills specifically needed for the operation of the business and through the successful application of this knowledge and skill. Skills were organized into various blocks, organized by degree of complexity, area of focus, and production department. The basic skill-block organization is outlined below.

Basic Operating Skills. The initial three employee pay levels (identified as Technician 1, 2, and 3) were designed with the goal of having each technician in the plant progress to a level of mastery of operating skills in the particular area he or she worked in. The intent was to build into the organization the understanding of its general operating purpose (production) with technicians beginning their careers by learning and mastering basic skills. All these skills would be developed and grown from within the organization, rather than through the hiring of outsiders. It was believed this would provide technicians and managers with the opportunity to begin the process of achieving an optimal fit between organizational needs and individual desires. Technicians would have some time to become socialized into the organization and would receive close counsel before having to decide on a personal career path. In addition, the mastery of basic operating skills would serve as a base on which further flexibility could be built into the technicians' jobs.

Administrative Skills. Plant O handled a variety of administrative requirements through the technician progression paths. The intent was to provide basic administrative skills to work teams on shifts and to minimize the need for clerical staff or large permanent staffs of maintenance personnel. It would also give technicians a wider exposure to other career alternatives as they began their process of selecting individual progression paths. Last, it would provide teams with a set of skills critical to their achieving a level of self-support.

Maintenance Skills and Operational Flexibility. A significant characteristic of the progression system was the flexibility it promoted. Technicians would cover a variety of job assignments as a function of the need at the time. This system enabled the production operations to shift with market requirements without incurring such major shifts in the workforce as large layoffs or expensive retraining. This flexibility was rooted in technicians with multiskills (either multioperational or maintenance, or both). In all operating areas, the job requirements were such that all technicians would develop both operating and maintenance skills independent of the particular career path they chose. The intent was to provide all operating technicians with some maintenance skills and all who chose maintenance careers with some operating skills. The result would be more broadly trained technicians, thereby lessening the need for pure, highly skilled specialists. In addition, maintenance skills would be built into individual-shift work teams.

Leadership Skills. The leadership skills blocks were designed to recognize and reward technicians for those skills generally considered to be supervisory, or leadership, in nature. The idea of developing leadership skills in the technician workforce was rooted in four design principles that had grown out of the open systems planning process[2] :

1) Push decisions to the lowest appropriate level at which the data is available to make those decisions. People who are impacted by a decision should have a voice in making them if they have the data.

2) Individuals should be given as much job responsibility as she/he is ready to handle. The jobs in Plant O should be meaningful and all employees should have the chance to grow to their full potential.

3) Work teams and the individuals on those teams are a whole unit, and are to carry out all those functions that are necessary to operate up to and including the leadership types of functions.

4) As teams and technicians develop and the system matures, teams can begin to operate without direct shift management/supervision for significant periods of time, i.e., the multiskilled team can operate the shift-to-shift and day-to-day, week-to-week type of routine activities. *This is not to say that Plant O can do away with manufacturing supervisors but as the teams evolve, mature, and grow, the manufacturing supervisors can evolve to a new role. A major part of that new role is dealing with the team on such responsibilities as team development, overall performance, team organizational problems, team planning and goals, communications, and employee relations type problems ranging from pay and progression and career development to discipline. The remainder of the supervisor's role then is to be free to work on department problems and projects that will move the business ahead.* (Italics Author's)

Four distinct levels of leadership were incorporated into the system:[3]

General. All technicians were expected to perform general leadership functions. These included responsibility for one's job, maintaining appropriate quality, safety, training, output, and participation. If experienced, the technician was expected to take charge of a group of other technicians to get something done.

Leadership I. This level formalized the development of skills necessary to plan and achieve results on a specific activity that had a defined end point of a limited scope. The intent of this level was for technicians to accomplish tasks in situations in which they had responsibility for a group of people.

Leadership II. At this level, the technician began to assume responsibility for leading a whole team for periods of time. This was usually accomplished under the guidance of a manufacturing supervisor for short periods of time up to a week in duration. The manufacturing supervisor was always to be available in a fallback position. At Leadership II, a technician might also have had a major responsibility for running a subportion of a team and the manufacturing process.

Leadership III. The Leadership III level called for a technician to be able to take over a manufacturing operation and its work team, in the absence of a manufacturing supervisor, for an extended period of time (three to six months). The technician was expected to handle all technical problems with the same poise and depth as a manufacturing supervisor. In administrative areas the technician was expected to be as able, but perhaps not as fast, as a manufacturing supervisor. In disciplinary situations, the technician was to be able to handle the bulk of what a manufacturing supervisor does, but to confirm his or her direction with management.

Training and Development

Extensive training was provided to all technicians at start-up. Three key components comprised the training effort: the use of technicians from other plants brought into Plant O on a short-term basis to serve as trainers; the sending of former XYZ Company employees to other plants for equipment training and then returning to Plant O as trainers; and a well-organized on-site equipment trainee-qualifying program.

Ongoing training efforts were based on the training requirements established in the various pay and progression systems.

All supervisor positions included training programs ranging from six to 12 weeks. A typical manufacturing supervisor-training program included activities in the following areas: plant orientation, employee relations, management development, technician systems, security and safety, team integration, concern for people as individuals, team administration, department orientation, developing group and individual effectiveness, setting and communicating work standards and goals, problem solving and priority setting, managing conflict and pressures, technical skills, and operating details. All levels of the Plant O hierarchy had resource persons assigned to assist the new manufacturing supervisor in completing training in the different areas.

Communications

Management had a strong desire to maintain a free and open communications network throughout the plant. A number of vehicles were designed to assist the communications flow.

Nonmanagement Meetings. Regular biweekly meetings of a rotating group of technician representatives were held with the plant manager. These meetings provided an opportunity for technicians to air problems and exchange information with the plant manager.

One-to-Ones. One-to-ones were scheduled between manufacturing supervisors and technicians every two to three months. These meetings were to be used for performance evaluations and feedback, problem sharing and solving, and relationship building.

Team Meetings. Thirty-minute team meetings were held on a daily basis at the beginning of each shift. These meetings were used broadly for information sharing, problem solving, training, and team building.

Bulletin Boards. Bulletin boards were used to post information initially shared through other (verbal) channels.

Clerical Work Team. The clerical and secretarial work team met weekly to exchange information and work on special projects.

In addition to these well-established channels of communication, a number of other meetings were held among management and various subgroups of the plant organization.

Hiring of Nonmanagerial Personnel

The hiring process was viewed essentially as a function of the line organization. An employment specialist would prescreen applications and then funnel potential job candidates to a pair of supervisors or other line managers, who would individually evaluate candidates against an established set of criteria (used corporate-wide) and then come to a joint determination regarding the individual's suitability for employment at Plant O. Whenever possible, candidates would be interviewed by those supervisors or managers who had the open spots, thereby attempting to increase the line organization's sense of ownership of the employment process.

At start-up, the available work records of former XYZ Company employees were used in addition to the interview procedure described above.

Availability of Plant Manager

A conscious decision was made to have the plant manager available to all levels of the Plant O organization. A number of the communications vehicles described serviced this intent. In addition, the plant manager held scheduled one-to-ones with all supervisors and managers every six months and maintained high levels of informal contact with technicians.

Work Schedules

A large majority of plant operations were scheduled on a seven-day-week, three-shift-a-day rotation. Work teams rotated shifts on a regular (seven- to ten-day) basis according to a southern-swing rotation commonly found in the paper industry. Manufacturing supervisors rotated with their teams.

Plant Operating Units

The plant was organized into three major operating units: paper-making, paper converting, and materials distribution. Each was under the supervision of a unit operations manager and contained one to three departments.

INTERNAL SOCIAL SYSTEM

The Supervisor's Role: Schedules and Team Meetings

As was outlined earlier, Plant O operated all the papermaking facilities and half the converting facilities on a seven-day-a-week, 24-hour-a-day basis. Each seven-day operation was staffed by four crews who would regularly rotate shifts in order to keep departments fully staffed. Manufacturing supervisors rotated shifts with their work teams. The remaining converting departments were staffed on a five-day, three-shift basis with three rotating crews. Shifts overlapped each other by a half hour each day in order to allow supervisors to conduct a team meeting at the start of each shift. These meetings were used broadly for information sharing, problem solving, training, and team building, and represented an additional investment of approximately 6 percent of direct labor costs. They were viewed with varying degrees of enthusiasm and skepticism by supervisors. Many of the college supervisors stated that preparation for a good team meeting required approximately one hour's investment in planning for it. Other supervisors were content to go through their mail 10 to 15 minutes before the meeting and pick out appropriate items to communicate to the team. Two or three supervisors viewed the team meeting as being analogous to a football coach's locker room pep talk. They looked to the meeting as a mechanism for psyching up the team before they took to the floor. In interviews, these supervisors maintained that the quality of the team meeting had a direct relationship with the way people would perform on the floor that day. One stated:

> I can tell whether or not we're going to have a good day from the team meeting. If people come in dragging their behinds and I can't perk them up, it's going to be like pulling teeth to get production. On the other hand, if they come in alert and kid around a lot in the meeting, we should do well.

Another supervisor reported:

> I'm not good at playing coach in the team meetings. Some of our supervisors are real good at it. I like to just talk to the people. So my team

meetings are not very exciting, and my team is a bit more low key, rational, and consistent than most others.

Span of Control, Administration, and Discipline

Supervisors maintained a span of control of over six to 40 people, with the smaller spans of control concentrated in papermaking and the larger crews in converting areas. This wide variation in crew size obviously had significant implications for the ways in which supervisors managed. Given the amount of administrative attention supervisors needed to pay to preparing individual training and pay and progression packages and to providing workers with regular one-to-one performance feedback, paper-converting supervisors were forced to delegate more of the shift-operating responsibilities to the team than were papermaking supervisors. In addition, operation of the paper machines required more of the specialized technical knowledge of the experienced supervisors than did the significantly less complex converting operations. It was interesting to note how supervisors used their administrative responsibilities as a major reward or sanction for performance. As one converting supervisor said:

> I tell them that if they take care of most of the daily production needs
> I get freed up to work on pay and progression packages for people. If
> I have to spend my time on the floor directly supervising their efforts
> I have less time to work on assisting employees to get their promo-
> tions and pay increases. This seems to get the message across.

Supervisors tended to rely on a documented counseling strategy in dealing with individual poor performance. A worker would be scheduled for a special one-to-one meeting in which he or she would be confronted with evidence of poor performance and asked if any problem was affecting performance for which the supervisor might be of assistance. A record of the discussion would be placed in the employee's file. Continued poor performance would lead to disciplinary action (time off without pay) up to and including dismissal. Most supervisors viewed disciplinary action as one of the most distasteful aspects of their job. One supervisor stated:

> I don't know whether to coach, coerce, or cajole poor performers.
> I often wonder whether I've adopted the right stance after the fact.

For example, I know I should fire some of my people but I just can't do it. I wish that I could be just like the father who kicks his kids in the rear and gets them to realize they're adults.

Supervisory Organization

As mentioned earlier, there was a deliberate mix of skills and backgrounds in the supervisory force, with the intent of fostering the exchange of knowledge through extensive interaction. Unfortunately, the seven-day work schedule precluded much interaction, with most supervisors generally interacting only with their departmental peers around the shift change and in a weekly department meeting.

Supervisors were expected to attend the weekly meetings even when held off their shift. Interviews with converting supervisors revealed dissatisfaction with the arrangement. One supervisor remarked:

> I can understand wanting to make sure that everyone gets communicated to so that we're all in the same boat but I've got better things to do than come in on my off shift for them. When I don't really want to be there in the first place the meetings end up being a waste of time.

The quality of supervisor interaction around shift change appeared to vary significantly with positive feelings from the continuity supervisor and relatively negative feelings from some of the younger supervisors. A continuity supervisor stated:

> Relations between us are real good. I'll always come in early to have a cup of coffee with the other supervisor before shift change, and whenever possible we socialize quite a bit.

While a college supervisor stated:

> Relations among the newer supervisors are all job oriented and are pretty shaky. There is a lot of competition and information hoarding. Every shift change brings on more complaints.

Relationships among the newer supervisors were undoubtedly affected by their desire for the rapid promotion that would enhance their careers and get them off shift work. The relatively poor relationships between continuity and college supervisors were correspondingly related to the feelings of several continuity supervisors who had promotional aspirations and who therefore resented being by-passed by people with less-developed skills and little experience.

Supervisor Know-How

There were substantial differences of opinion among supervisors and managers in Plant O regarding the extent to which supervisors had to be technically proficient. At the supervisory level you could find people saying:

> I'm probably at a Tech level 2 if you want to compare me with hourly operators. But I designed my job that way. I don't groove on sprockets and grease. I need to know enough to troubleshoot. I will admit, however, if I had greater competence my start-up would have been easier.

> I'm at a Tech 4 or 5 level and would expect that after 12 to 15 months on the floor my technicians should be able to teach me.

> They can't snow me. I learned all I need to know to do the job and would rate myself as a Tech 2.

Other supervisors were saying:

> My technical competence is super high and it's really helped me to develop my crew.

> We'll have new supervisors sitting in their offices doing reports or one-on-ones while the machine is in a pile. They couldn't help out if they wanted to.

There appeared to be several explanatory factors for the disagreements regarding the importance of developing technical skills. First was the awareness that papermaking required a technical level of sophistication that exceeded the level on converting operations. Second was the composition of the supervisory group. Four of the nine supervisors interviewed were promoted to their positions from an hourly position at Plant O or elsewhere and had assumed their positions with substantial papermaking experience. These supervisors generally felt strongly about the need for technical skills. Most of the college-educated supervisors placed a greater emphasis on the interpersonal skills they relied on to get the job done and played down the technical demands of the job. Lastly, a supervisor's feelings were often rooted in the expressed opinions of their superiors. As an operations manager put it:

> Our first college supervisors had credibility problems on the floor. Those who didn't pick up technical skills were "dropped" by the Team.

A department manager stated:

> The supervisor must know at least the technical basics as well as have a good problem-solving ability or we end up with fewer cases.

Another department manager summed it up this way:

> In recruiting new supervisors, I look more for an ability to learn technical processes. The interpersonal skills are easier to pick up.

It was clear that Plant O had a base level of technical competence required to carry out the supervisor's job responsibilities with room for wide variation in a supervisor's overall technical ability.

Supervisor Responsibility and Accountability

Within this area we saw the substantial impact of the technician system on the supervisor's role. Not only was the Plant O supervisor accountable for achieving hard-number results (e.g., production, scrap, yield, efficiency) but he or she had to continue to manage the unique demands that the Plant O concept of operation placed on all supervisors: administration of pay and progression systems, one-to-one meetings, career development discussions, conducting daily team meetings, and so on. Supervisors uniformly expressed their feelings about the magnitude of the demands placed on them:

> The expectations of me within the plant are incredible and the wages are relatively low.

> If a supervisor is to be successful he's got to be able to funnel pressure and responsibility down to the floor.

> The amount of hours we have to put in are unbelievable. I'd be a lot better financially as a technician.

> When this was an XYZ plant I was only responsible for production. Now with my enormous administrative duties my job load is doubled.

Department and unit operations managers were clear in their expectation that supervisors address themselves to issues that transcended the traditional notion of the supervisors' role. A unit operations manager stated:

> We expect our supervisors to take a broader view of their work and to get involved with higher level concerns. They should be involved in personnel decision making, special projects, and departmental planning if they are to get ahead.

Yet at the same time, in the words of one unit operations manager:

> Our lead technicians are not supervisors and we still need them.

The demands placed on the supervisors were not unlike the demands that, as a group of aggressive, career-oriented managers, Plant O management placed on themselves. This is how two managers expressed their views on the topic. A unit operations manager complained:

> We suffer from a "be-perfect" syndrome. It's not ok for us to feel good about what we've done. We just move on toward the next milestone. And the brunt of the burden falls on the supervisor.

And a department manager said:

> We respond very quickly to upsets. In fact, sometimes we respond too quickly to simple blips. For example, it is absolutely inexcusable for a supervisor to have had a bad day and not understand why or do anything about it.

One of the apparent keys to supervisory success was the ability to diffuse responsibilities among the technicians and to have them perform an increased proportion of the area's required activities and functions. This took a great deal of time and effort on the part of the supervisor.

There appeared to be two predominant ways in which the supervisor diffused responsibility for results: First, through the use of social and interpersonal skills, the supervisor successfully assisted in the process of team development and continually funneled portions of the workload down to the technicians. Second, the pay and progression system was slowed down to recognize poor performance. Promotions were minimal and additional training was held back.

Supervisor Communications

Communications with Management

A variety of mechanisms were available to supervisors to communicate with management. The general conclusion from supervisors about their relationship with management was that "people are always there when you need them and sometimes even when you don't!"

Scheduled one-to-ones were held between a supervisor and the department manager approximately once a month, between the supervisor and the unit operations manager once every two to three months, and between the supervisor and the plant manager once every six months. Each of these meetings was designed to update the supervisor with feedback on his or her performance and to allow the supervisor to air any issues or concerns — generally the issues supervisors raised appeared to be around pay or career development.

Both managers and supervisors regarded one-to-ones as a valuable management tool. Since different one-to-ones occurred between the supervisor and each of the levels of the organization, half the supervisors interviewed indicated the importance of recognizing and respecting the hierarchy in terms of information flow:

> It is extremely important that you pay attention to the chain of command and not have lower-level managers surprised by information you provide to the unit operations or plant manager. That can really backfire on you.

Production meetings were held each morning to review the previous day's performance and to design plans for dealing with any problem areas. These meetings generally included the department manager, maintenance manager, third and first shift supervisors, and the first shift lead technician. The meetings were regarded as helpful by all parties involved. At the meeting, the supervisors often found themselves having to provide answers to questions about occurrences on the floor that contributed to less-than-satisfactory performance:

> Just knowing that I have to have answers tomorrow morning keeps me out on the floor more than I really should be. I really can't hold my lead technician accountable.

One problem identified by a number of supervisors was a perceived emphasis on written communications. College supervisors generally responded positively to the emphasis:

> I write a weekly letter, and it really helps to keep people informed.

> I write six-month game plans and send them around. I think it's really helped my career here.

But continuity supervisors responded quite negatively:

> They keep saying I've got to do more writing. If I spent the time necessary to do the writing I couldn't manage the floor properly.

> It's just as easy to listen to what I have to say but the operations manager insists on us writing.

Communications with Hourly Employees

In addition to the daily team meeting, one-to-ones were held with each employee every one to three months. One supervisor's general agenda for one-to-ones, known throughout the plant, included the following questions: How do you feel about my expectations of you? What expectations do you have of me? What problems have you (or your team) been having? Do you have a solution? How can I help? Where are you in pay and progression? What skills have you completed? What skills are you working on? What problems do you have? What are you like? How do you feel about the team? Century Corporation? Your job?

Other supervisors used agendas that appeared to be much less formal and more tailored to the individual employee.

About half the supervisors were unsure of the cost/benefit trade-offs associated with the time they spent in one-to-one meetings:

> I don't really think they're all that worthwhile. I do them when I get pressure from my boss because I know that it's a top-management priority item.

> I prefer to talk to people on the line.

The remaining supervisors were certain of the benefits of conducting one-to-ones.

Supervisor/technician communications and relationships could be characterized as ranging from adequate to absolutely superb. An operations manager characterized one end of the continuum:

> We have one supervisor who's like a god to the people. They'll do any-thing for him and he's really developed them.

The supervisor in question commented:

> I just spend a lot of time on the floor. First, I'll show a technician something, second I'll do it with him, and then he's on his own. I just treat them the way I like to be treated.

Supervisor Goal Setting and Motivating

Goals around operating results were set on the unit and depart-mental levels. They were then passed down to supervisors who were assigned the task of leading their teams through a goal-setting process. Supervisors generally reacted to the team goal-setting process with some skepticism:

> We set goals but it's a game. I know the numbers we have to come up with. But I guess the technicians kind of enjoy it.

> We influence the teams to come up with our numbers. Some people are getting wise to the process.

> Most goals and standards are laid on us by top management — pure and simple.

Management placed a great deal of emphasis on supervisors setting standards, establishing expectations, and holding technicians accountable. In conjunction with this emphasis there was a strong norm that called for written documentation of interchanges with employees around standards and goals.

One of the more successful supervisors (in the eyes of upper management) summed up his approach to goal setting and motivation in the following manner:

> It's very simple. We *will* be #1 in all areas.

The skills-based pay and progression system for technicians was intended to serve as a key motivating force for skills acquisition and application. It was also the primary vehicle used for purposes of controlling and gauging the development of people and teams. It appeared to be critical to the success of Plant O supervisors that pay and progression be managed efficiently and fairly:

> If I screw up on pay and progression, I'm taking money out of someone's pocket and they are rightfully teed off.

Supervisor as Trainer

Given the emphasis management attached to the acquisition and development of a variety of skills by the technicians, it was surprising at first that there appeared to be significant differences in the importance the supervisors attached to their role as trainers of technicians. These differences appeared to be primarily rooted in the capabilities and skills that supervisors themselves brought to the job and in their desire to get involved in training activities. For example, here is a typical comment from one of the highly skilled continuity supervisors:

> I spend a lot of time doing training with people on the machine and get heavily involved with their qualifications.

One of the more recent college supervisors presented a different picture when she stated:

I do very little technical training and never have. Whatever skills training goes on is one-to-one with the best operator available. My job is to make sure that the training happens.

Virtually all the supervisors, however, indicated that they spent a good deal of time in a training relationship with the higher-level technicians, particularly in the area of developing leadership, motivation, and other management skills.

The plant design appeared to allow for flexibility of choice in personal definitions of the training role of the supervisor. A training center and a variety of available resource persons all supported the supervisor who chose not to get heavily involved in a direct training effort.

Supervisor as Planner

Century Corporation had a widespread reputation as a particularly thorough planning company. And Plant O did nothing to injure this reputation. However, in considering the changing role of the supervisor as teams developed self-direction capacity, there appeared to be some indication of an uncharacteristic wait-and-see attitude among top managers exemplified by the following quote by an operations manager:

Who knows what will happen [to the supervisor role]? We'll let things evolve and we'll tackle problems as they arise.

Another operations manager outlined what he saw as the implications of the Plant O technician system for the supervisor's role:

1. Ultimately fewer supervisor positions would be available.
2. The supervisory force would contain a heavier proportion of continuity supervisors.
3. New supervisors would be technically stronger with more experience.
4. More new college recruits would begin their careers in staff positions rather than as supervisors.

He continued:

We'll just let it happen as it comes up. I don't see any great need to plan for it.

In a corresponding vein, supervisors did not appear to do much long-range planning relative to their role vis-a-vis the teams. A typical supervisor response was:

> We're so overloaded now, who has time to think about three to five years out?

This lack of planning was further exacerbated by the short-term nature of the assignment for most college-educated supervisors. With most initial supervisor assignments of a one- to three-year duration, the implications of any reconceptualization was not of direct concern to them.

Much of the supervisor's time was taken up in day-to-day reactions to on-the-floor production pressures. This further constrained any attempt at planning of a long-term nature. As one supervisor stated:

> Trying to plan beyond the week is like spitting in the ocean.

The only planning of a longer-term nature that supervisors engaged in was associated with administration of the pay and progression system. The supervisor had to map out training and promotion schedules for the teams on a three- to six-month basis. Most of these plans did not appear to be formally spelled out in writing. One supervisor remarked:

> I believe I'm the only supervisor with a formal written six-month game plan which gets updated every month. It's been a helpful exercise for me and has served as some good public relations for me.

ORGANIZATIONAL OUTCOMES: SUPERVISORY SATISFACTION AND EFFECTIVENESS

As a group, the supervisors in Plant O are perceived as being quite effective. They ranked as the most effective supervisory workforce in our case studies of plants (Appendix). They were evaluated as having strong organizational, technical, and professional skills. Although their interpersonal skills were evaluated as being significantly less well developed than their other skills, Plant O supervisors again ranked highest in our sample of plants.

Given our description of Plant O and Century Corporation's commitment to the development of management talent these findings are not surprising. One would expect that the management of this plant would tolerate nothing less than a highly competent supervisory workforce.

At the same time, given the pressures incumbent on supervisors at Plant O, it is not surprising that they ranked third out of the four plants studied, in terms of job satisfaction and held the most negative attitudes toward plant management recorded in our study.

FEEDBACK AND RENEWAL SYSTEMS

In our review of the many communications vehicles designed as a formal part of Plant O operations, it became obvious that there were many opportunities for supervisors and managers to receive and process information on the internal social system and organizational outcomes.

The plant manager's work team served as the primary tool for organizational analysis and action planning and implementation on issues that cut across departmental boundaries or that were plant-wide in scope. Decisions made at this level were funneled down to the appropriate organizational level for implementation and were monitored by the individual unit operations managers.

No similar vehicle existed for supervisors. Supervisor concerns and problems appear to be worked through hierarchical channels on an individual, or at most, a departmental basis. Outside of an occasional formal training program, no systematic mechanism existed to bring the manufacturing supervisors together as a group.

ANALYSIS OF THE SUPERVISOR SITUATION

Let us use the model outlined in Chapter 2 to assist us in understanding the supervisory situation as it exists in Plant O. Plant O presented us with a picture of a supervisory workforce that appeared to be highly competent, yet many of the supervisors were dissatisfied with their jobs. How can we begin to explain these contrasting outcomes?

Supervisor-Organizational Design. The Plant O organizational design was oriented toward providing the worker with an opportunity for challenge and satisfaction on the job and an attractive pay package by community standards. The design clearly went a long way toward anticipating and meeting worker needs.

However, there appeared to be little evidence of similar attention to the needs of supervisors in the organizational design. In fact, many of the design elements in place at Plant O appeared to increase the demands placed on the supervisory role, for example, the requirements of managing the pay and progression system or of conducting a daily team meeting. All appearances are that Plant O began their design effort by implicitly assuming that their supervisors would do everything all other Century Corporation supervisors did plus assume additional responsibilities as dictated by the worker-oriented organizational design.

Given the supervisors' workload, it is not surprising that we uncovered no complaints that supervisors were interfering with technicians doing their jobs, a complaint common to many of the other plants we studied.

Supervisor-Key Tasks and Technologies. Earlier, we characterized the variety of technologies that comprised Plant O operations and highlighted their critical interdependences. It was clear from our study that the supervisory group presented a broad continuum of technical expertise on the job (from unable to be "snowed" to high technical competence), and this significantly influenced the way in which they related to their technicians.

At the same time, the supervisory force exhibited a wide spectrum of competence in carrying out the administrative aspects of their job (e.g., report writing, one-to-ones, training schedules). This, too, had an impact on their performance in these areas.

In the absence of any clear definition of roles and responsibilities, supervisors exhibited a natural tendency to work to their strengths and to minimize their involvement in areas they were weak in. Our observations and interviews presented a picture of continuity and up-from-the-ranks supervisors investing the bulk of their energy in technical issues and the college supervisors paying significantly more attention to managing administrative issues.

This created, between the two groups, inevitable tensions that, at the time of our study, had neither surfaced nor been addressed. Those managers who emphasized the technical aspects of their job tended to spend more time on the production floor and to perceive their on-the-floor presence as a factor that improved production. They observed the college-educated supervisors spending time writing reports or in one-to-ones, while there were technical problems on the floor; they were unable to deal with this different job definition. They also watched college supervisors get promoted to managerial positions, and over time began to question their own value in the system. They worked long hours, received no overtime pay, had no career prospects beyond their current level in the organization, and perceived the promotion of many of the college-educated supervisors as a direct attack on the significance of their own technical competence.

At the same time, the college-educated supervisors talked about the need to manage the process of the team toward self-direction; they saw little reason to intervene in day-to-day on-the-floor actions, unless they were receiving pressure for information relating to less-than-satisfactory performance.

Supervisor-Internal Social System. In terms of their relationship with management on a day-to-day basis, supervisors were barraged with a multitude of messages regarding actions they should be taking. In the morning meeting they might be held accountable for poor production results the preceding day and have to outline a technical action plan for resolving any problems. An hour later, they might be confronted for failure to complete one-to-ones on time or be requested to prepare a written report of their activities over the past month. In short, the supervisor was expected to juggle a large number of balls; in the Plant O environment, a supervisor could expect to be questioned as soon as he or she let one drop.

The situation created an inevitable defensiveness among supervisors when interacting with management and served as a prime source of supervisor discontent. At the same time management claimed to recognize the issue and maintained that effective supervisors must juggle all the balls, just as managers in the Plant O environment did.

In terms of their relationship with workers and work teams, it was not surprising that we found a symbiotic relationship. Work teams tended to defer any significant operating decisions to a strong technical supervisor, independent of the work team's state of development. With a weak technical supervisor, the work team worked to resolve operating problems themselves and to update the supervisor on the floor or to inform the supervisor after the issue had been worked out. In either event, it was recognized that, independent of the supervisor's involvement in resolving an operating problem, the supervisor had to be kept thoroughly informed to ensure that he or she had information should management request it.

Key Tasks and Technologies-Organizational Design. The pay and progression system, probably the cornerstone of the Plant O organizational design, serviced not only individual needs, but was designed to support plant operations with a multiskilled and highly flexible workforce. It performed that function well. The system appeared to motivate people to develop a variety of skills, through the financial incentives it provided.

Key Tasks and Technologies-Internal Social System. The symbiotic relationship between supervisors and work teams outlined earlier contributed to task accomplishment in a highly efficient and effective way.

Organizational Design-Internal Social System. The insistence of management that supervisors maintain ultimate resonsibility and accountability for on-the-floor results appeared to inhibit any lasting work group self-direction, one of the explicit goals of the pay and progression system. At the same time, this pressure for results did appear to yield good business results.

In the absence of any clarity in their job description and in any planning for their future role in the organization, supervisors (especially those who fell into the continuity category) recognized the need to get good numbers. As one supervisor remarked:

> We've got to do everything around here. But if our production is good the pressure on us to get the other work done isn't as great. If our numbers fall, they can lower the boom in all areas though.

At the same time, no provisions were made to allow supervisors as a group to share, and attempt to work through, the ambiguities and frustrations of their job. Their discontent could only be shared among a small nucleus of supervisors (those on the same shift, and those he or she relieved or was relieved by). Inevitably, a sizable portion of this nucleus consisted of college supervisors, making it difficult for continuity supervisors to have someone to share with, or vice versa.

SUMMARY

Century Corporation's Plant O opted, in practice, for an operating system that allowed for the development of individual worker skills so as to maximize the plant's flexibility in the allocation of personnel. The pay and progression system stood as the cornerstone of their participative operations.

Plant O's notions of worker self-direction were restricted in focus to skill flexibility and minor decision making on the floor during routine production schedules. Technicians, for the most part, were very tightly monitored and controlled by the manufacturing supervisors, who were held accountable for all that occurred on the production floor. All operating goals of significance were developed at the managerial level and were set forth for employees through a series of team goal-setting exercises conducted by the supervisors.

The pay and progression system placed an enormous load on the supervisory workforce to administer it both correctly and equitably. Errors in administration often led to employee disaffection and additional personnel problems for the supervisor to address. Unfortunately for the supervisor, this responsibility, as well as many others, did not replace any traditional responsibilities that he or she had been able to relinquish as a result of the plant's participative mode of operation. Supervisors continued to be directly responsible for day-to-day results. They had to be able to respond to superiors on a daily basis regarding the previous day's events, as well as explain their actions regarding any production time lost on their shift. Supervisors continued to fill out attendance reports, to handle clerical activities regarding payroll, and to perform many other traditional supervisory functions.

In practice, Plant O management has addressed the question of the supervisory role by adding, rather than replacing or substituting, responsibilities to the supervisory role. A substantial majority of the supervisory force at Plant O believe they are overworked and underpaid, with no overtime compensation for supervisors at Plant O. Furthermore, improvements in the quality of work life for hourly employees appear to have come largely at the supervisor's expense, an example being the technicians' benefits associated with the pay and progression system requiring more of a supervisor's personal time.

For those who assumed the supervisory role straight out of college, the job was seen as a short-term paying of dues, for assignment would generally last no more than three years. They undertook the additional responsibilities with greater enthusiasm than did the average continuity supervisors. In fact, it was generally recognized that the length of time a college recruit spent in the supervisory position was most often related to how well he or she performed in the position. Therefore, it was clearly in their best interests to attack the job with as much energy as possible, to put in whatever time was necessary for successful completion of the job, to document their activities to superiors on a regular basis, and to hope a new position became available soon.

The situation for continuity managers was quite different. The possibility of moving off shifts to another job was not a realistic option for this group. Consequently, they were less willing to perform the additional administrative tasks imposed by Plant O's mode of operation. Given the differences in orientation and career opportunities for these two groups of supervisors, it was not surprising to find strains in their relationships with each other.

The clear-cut responsibilities, the sound organizational design, the highly competent and aggressive management group, and the state-of-the-art technology, combined with a host of other factors, led to highly positive business outcomes at Plant O. The misfits between many of the elements highlighted led to much of the dissatisfaction and discontent expressed by the supervisors at Plant O.

As we looked at the Plant O organization, however, we found little evidence of any of the elements evolving toward a state that could inhibit the capacity of the plant to change the role of the supervisor to one that was perceived more positively by the occupants of the role.

NOTES

1. Internal company document, 1974.
2. Internal company document, 1975.
3. Internal company document, 1975.

4

Case Study: Plant G

OVERVIEW OF THE PLANT

One of five plants that comprised the ball bearings division of the National Corporation, Plant G was part of a large, highly diversified company headquartered in the Midwest.* With its capacity for high-volume production, it was designed to service the growing demand for commercial-grade ball bearings products, a major item in National's product line. The plant was built in 1974 and started up in 1975.

Plant G was located in a small southeastern town approximately 60 miles from a major metropolitan area. The primary employers in the community were based in farming, poultry processing, and textiles manufacturing, leaving Plant G as the first machining industry in the area. A major reason for locating in the community was the incentives provided by the state for new industry. Most

---

*All identifications relating to the plant and to the company have been disguised.

73

notable of these incentives was a state-funded training facility and training program for new employees. National's management also considered a small town location attractive, in that the local population would tend to exhibit a greater commitment to the town and companies in it.

At the time of this study (March 1977) the plant employed approximately 280 people distributed across a three-shift, seven-day operation.

INTEREST IN CREATING A PARTICIPATIVE WORK SYSTEM

The National Corporation, which acquired the ball bearings division in 1973, was a recognized leader in the application of human relations and behavioral science concepts to the workplace. Over the past 15 years the division had recognized substantial growth, largely attributable to its position as the technological leader in the domestic bearings industry. Increasingly, however, foreign competition had posed threats to domestic manufacturers on both the price and technological fronts.

Concerns over foreign competition placed additional pressures on division management to develop an outstandingly productive plant. For a number of years, other divisions of National, with the support and encouragement of corporate resources, had engaged in a variety of activities aimed at increasing both employee productivity and worker satisfaction. An internal document outlined the intent of these activities:

> The objectives are substantial improvements in organizational effectiveness, employee productivity, and the individual's quality of work experience. We expect to realize improvements of at least 10 percent and will be placing emphasis on situations where 20-40 percent improvements appear to be possible. These improvements result from a combination of changes which vary from project based on the specific opportunities and leverage points in each situation. These improvements include higher yields, less waste, better utilization of equipment through more continuous operation/less downtime, higher quality, substantially more problem-solving at the operator or first level, coupled with significantly less operational fire-fighting by managers (providing them with more time for analysis and planning, implementing long-term objectives, etc.); smaller work force, fewer levels

of supervision, less indirect staff and support personnel; lower turnover and absenteeism, and less demotivation and more personal fulfillment.

The management of Plant G looked to these activities as the base on which to build a model ball bearings plant. The management team was in place well in advance of the scheduled plant start-up and was afforded the opportunity to design the plant from scratch, with few limits on creativity and innovativeness.

Plant G became the first plant in the division to make major use of internal and external behavioral science resources in their planning activities. The plant manager, his six key subordinates, and the behavioral scientists met during the summer of 1974 to work through the details of the plant design and to prepare for a successful start-up. Each member of the Plant G management team was optimistic about his or her ability to institute a number of workplace innovations on a plantwide basis.

KEY TASKS AND TECHNOLOGIES[1]

The process involved in manufacturing commercial-grade ball bearings was a relatively capital-intensive technology. Major capital equipment investments were required for machinery to perform a number of complex metal-cutting and metal-grinding operations, for furnaces to heat-treat intermediate products, for materials handling and parts storage facilities, and for various auxiliary services that were necessary to operate and maintain the production equipment. Figure 4.1 displays a flow chart that outlines the various steps in the production process.

The quality standards for commercial-grade ball bearings require a higher level of precision and greater attention to detail during the manufacturing process than do most types of mechanical products. The overall quality of a particular bearing depends on the accuracy of the dimensions of its component parts and on the quality of the surface finish on rolling-contact surfaces. Typically, the dimensions of a finished, commercial-grade ball bearing have to be machined to tolerances of 0.0005 of an inch. It was very important that parts be produced within specified tolerances at each step in the production process. If poor-quality parts were produced in the initial machining operations, it would become difficult — if not impossible

FIGURE 4.1
Flow Chart of the Production Process at Plant G

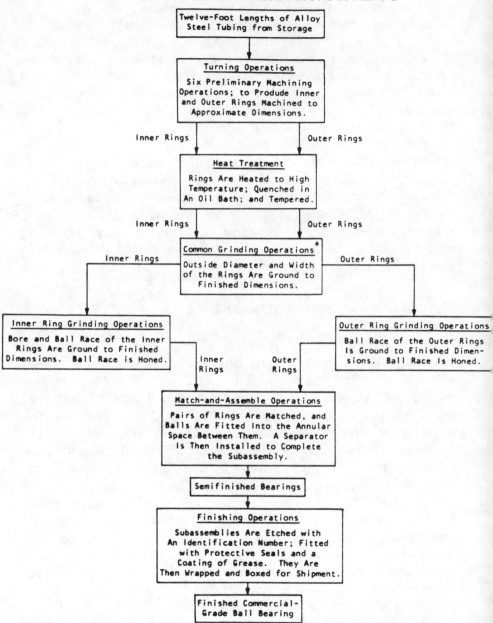

*Commonly referred to in the industry as "Hard Surface and O.D." operations.

— to machine parts to the correct, finished dimensions in subsequent operations. For those operations downstream in the process, where parts were to be machined to finished dimensions, the cost of rejecting out-of-tolerance parts was relatively high because of the value-added factor during previous machining and processing.

The level of operator skill was an important factor in determining overall productivity levels within the plant. Operators of the ball bearings production machinery had to be alert, possess good manual dexterity, and have a keen intuitive sense of technical know-how. An important part of the operator's job was to keep the machines in adjustment so that they would continue to produce within tolerance levels. In order to do this, the operator had to be able to determine which of many possible adjustments was necessary before making the required change. This kind of trouble-shooting ability was an important aspect of an experienced operator's skill. In addition, operators had to determine the point at which machine tools and grinding wheels ought to be changed in order to maintain quality. A skilled operator would make these decisions by balancing quality considerations against the high cost of retooling.

The cost of scrap materials, the level of work-in-process inventories, and the extent of machine utilization were other important factors affecting productivity and per-unit cost.

The cost of scrap materials (out-of-tolerance parts or bearings that had to be rejected) varied considerably from one plant to another. A minimum amount of raw material was unavoidably lost in the course of normal machining operations. This minimum level was relatively fixed and could be attained in plants using the latest proven technology, as was the case at Plant G. In capital-intensive plants, such as Plant G, utilization of the production machinery was also a major determinant of productivity. One factor that affected the amount of time machines were actually operating was the operators' skill level and interest in their work. Also, proper maintenance of the machinery and the ability to make repairs quickly could substantially reduce costly downtime and keep the machines operating consistently. Although this was a capital-intensive technology, commercial-grade ball bearings plants (including National's other plants) have traditionally operated on a basic five-day workweek with three shifts per day. Plant G's seven-day work schedule represented a significant departure from the practice.

INDIVIDUAL CHARACTERISTICS OF HUMAN RESOURCES

Supervisors

Table 4.1 presents an overview of the composition of Plant G's supervisory force.

Of the 12 manufacturing supervisors, only one-third had either previous industry experience or previous supervisory experience, or both. Two supervisors were promoted from the hourly or administrative workforce at other division plants.

There were no plantwide-defined criteria for the selection of supervisors. Candidates for supervisory positions were interviewed by virtually all members of the management staff, and hiring decisions were made on the basis of three criteria: (1) the gut feelings of the managers who conducted the interviews as to the suitability of the candidate for work in Plant G, given the type of plant they were trying to establish; (2) work history; and (3) reference checks. As we can see, this process resulted in a supervisory force having no clearly definable characteristics, other than being overwhelmingly male. Supervisors varied considerably in age, experience, and education.

The supervisors who were transferred from other division plants were expected to bring extensive manufacturing expertise that would be quite valuable during the start-up period.

Individual supervisors expressed surprise at the lack of definition provided for the supervisor's job at Plant G. One supervisor remarked:

> When I interviewed here, everyone kept asking me what I thought the job was. No one here really seemed to know.

Workers

The Plant G workforce was drawn primarily from an area concentrated within 25 miles of the plant. The selection process took place in three steps. First, the personnel department handled all initial employee applications and conducted screening interviews. Second, approximately one-third of the applicants progressed beyond the screening interview for an invitation to participate in a three-week introductory training program conducted off the plant site at the local technical school. The training was conducted in

TABLE 4.1
Composition of Plant G Supervisory Force

Employee	Sex	Age	Previous Ball Bearings Industry Experience (years)	Previous Supervisory Experience (years)	College
1	M	31	None	8½	None
2*	M	49	24	None	Currently attending
3	M	53	None	15	None
4	M	26	None	None	B.S., Engineering Management
5*	M	58	36	11	None
6	M	31	None	None	B.A.
7	M	30	None	None	M.S., Industrial Education
8	M	30	None	None	B.S., Technical Training
9*	M	46	25	5	None
10	M	29	None	None	None
11*	M	28	2	None	A.S., Engineering
12	F	28	None	None	None

*Transfer from another plant in the division.

79

morning, afternoon, and evening sessions to accommodate people who were employed elsewhere, and no compensation was provided for the participants. Thirty to 35 percent of the participants withdrew their applications for employment during this period. Finally, after successfully completing the voluntary introductory training program, the applicant was placed on the company payroll.

The voluntary introductory training program played a significant role in shaping the composition of the Plant G workforce. The exposure to what most applicants found to be a foreign technology, as well as the attention paid during the training period to human relations skills tended to force many to self-select out of the plant. Most of those applicants who did become employees had been attracted to the participative notions expressed during training. As one manager remarked:

> We've got a number of workers who've been canned from other places for telling off the boss. Here we encourage them to speak their piece, and they do.

The flexibility of the work system plus the opportunity to speak their piece was continually noted by employees as one of the major attractions of working at Plant G.

The workforce was approximately 15 percent female and 20 percent black. Most employees had a high school education; a small minority had some advanced technical or postgraduate training.

Managers

The Plant G plant manager was appointed in May 1974. His first task was to select a group of managers who would work with him. He selected five managers — four engineers and an accountant — all of whom had been working at another plant in the division at which the Plant G plant manager had most recently worked. The plant manager commented on the selection process for managers:

> I knew them all — they'd worked for me in _____ . I wouldn't say I had specific criteria. It was just one of those things where I knew they were the ones I wanted, without sitting down and writing out a bunch of criteria. It was sort of an informal type of thing. I pretty much had free choice of who I wanted.

During the first year of the plant's operation, one of the managers brought down to Plant G relocated to his home community and was replaced by a local hire; a local person was selected as the employee relations supervisor, as management considered it important that someone with a knowledge of the local community fill this position at start-up. In addition, in the fall of 1976 an outsider was hired to fill a newly defined position of organizational development manager. Table 4.2 provides an overview of the composition of the managerial workforce.

ORGANIZATIONAL DESIGN

Management Structure

Plant G operated with a straightforward functional structure at start-up. Each of the functional managers reported to the plant manager with the supervisors (three each for day, evening, and night shifts) reporting to the manufacturing manager. The start-up structure is outlined in Figure 4.2.

After three months of operation, supervisors were assigned to a portion of the production process (e.g., turning, heat-treat) rather than to a specific shift, for reasons we shall explore later.

In October 1976, an additional level of management was introduced into Plant G with the creation of two unit manager positions. Reporting to the manufacturing managers, each unit manager had six shift managers (from October 1975 to October 1976, three additional supervisors were hired) working for them and had coordination responsibility for a number of the operating areas. We shall explore the rationale behind this move in the next section of the report.

Production requirements, product specifications, and marketing plans were developed at division headquarters and were implemented through consultation with each of the plants.

Operating Mechanisms: The Team Concept

The design process employed by the Plant G management team resulted in the adoption of a team concept of operation modeled after a series of experiments recently conducted at the plant that the plant management team came from.

TABLE 4.2
Background Information on Plant Management Team Personnel

Employee	Age	Education	Years with National's Ball Bearings Division	Most Recent Work Assignment	Title at Plant G
1	51	B.S., M.S., Mechanical Engineering, University of Michigan	28	Works manager at two other plants	Plant manager
2	43	High school, 3 years college	Hired 10/75	Development engineer for tool and die company, Atlanta	Materials, EDP manager
3	46	B.B.A., Industrial Relations, University of Georgia	Hired 3/75	Plant personnel manager for a local plant of a national company	Employee relations manager
4	25	B.S., Industrial Engineering, Pennsylvania State University	4	Senior industrial engineer at another National plant	Industrial engineering manager

5	31	High school and approximately 1 year college credit	10	Senior industrial engineer at another National plant	Plant engineer
6	47	High school	20	Industrial engineering supervisor at another National plant	Manufacturing manager
7	33	Graduate, Jamestown Community College and additional courses	8	Division financial analyst at another National plant	Accounting manager
8	33	Ed.M., Organizational Behavior, Harvard University	Hired 10/76	Graduate student	Organizational development manager

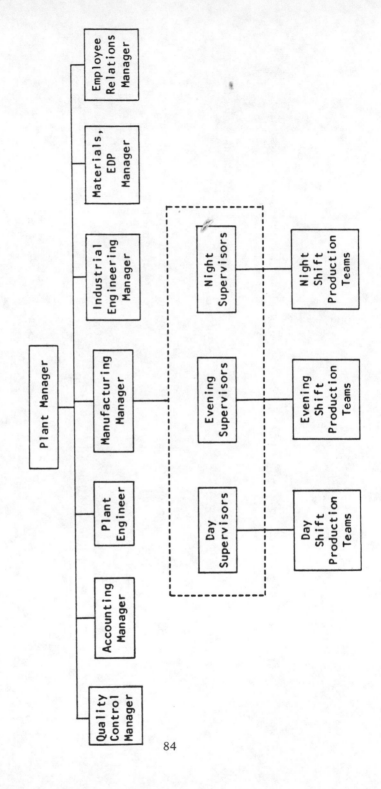

FIGURE 4.2
Start-up Organization Chart of Plant G – 1975

The team concept called for all the tasks necessary to operate Plant G, including maintenance and other production support functions, to be included among the responsibilities of a number of production teams consisting of eight to 25 persons. For example, in one production area, teams were assigned the responsibility for day-to-day production planning, machine repair and maintenance, quality control, and cleanup. The management team believed that by assigning teams an enriched, more challenging variety of tasks, job satisfaction, flexibility, and effectiveness would be increased.

One feature of the team concept that was especially attractive to management was that the team concept provided a natural setup for continuous, seven-day operation. They simply added 40 percent more people to the basic number required for each team and assigned production teams the responsibility for deciding who would work which five days. Prior to start-up, the managers did not decide whether the teams would always work the same shift or would be rotated across shifts. Nor did they resolve the question of whether individuals or whole teams should be rotated if they went to a rotating shift schedule. At start-up, it was decided that each team would be permanently assigned to one shift, until February 1, 1977, by which time workers and management would have worked out a plan whereby workers would be assigned to shifts. Management believed this arrangement would provide the substantial economic benefits of continuous operation, with few administrative complications. As a direct result of the decision to adopt the team concept, management increased shipping and sales commitments for the new plant by 40 percent, thereby increasing Plant G's projected return on investment substantially through the increased use of expensive capital equipment.

Once the basic team concept was agreed upon, management completed the basic design. The team concept provided a framework for resolving a number of other issues requiring immediate attention: plant layout, a compensation system, a plan for supervising the teams, and a plan for training new employees. This framework assisted management in developing a formal set of design objectives, which expressed their view of the team concept in some detail. These objectives represented a concrete expression of the project team's basic philosophy for designing and managing Plant G. Figure 4.3 exhibits the game plan.

FIGURE 4.3
Plant G: Design Objectives

Effectively optimize the building design, plant layout, materials handling, manufacturing equipment, and human resources to achieve a plant capable of high production, uniform high quality, low cost, and flexibility.

Building Design. The building has been designed to handle the sophisticated support facilities required in the manufacture of bearings, at the same time providing a desirable work environment for employees, including controlled atmosphere and temperature, adequate lighting, employee meeting rooms, cafeteria with picnic and recreation area, and finishes and design throughout the plant to facilitate housekeeping.

Plant Layout. The plant is laid out to ensure efficient flow of the product through the plant, at the same time ensuring proximity of members of production teams and equalizing and minimizing the travel of all employees to service and human support areas.

Materials Handling. The materials handling system is being designed to ensure smooth parts flow and sufficient parts storage. Also, the system is being designed to reduce or eliminate the physical labor required to move material, as well as to facilitate housekeeping in the plant.

Manufacturing Equipment. Manufacturing equipment selected is the most advanced proven method of manufacturing bearing races available. The equipment is designed to be able to hold the exacting tolerances required with a minimum of adjustment. Much of the tooling is being redesigned to facilitate machine setups and operation. Machines are equipped to meet OSHA standards, lower noise levels, and eliminate air pollution, to produce a more desirable work environment.

Human Resources. In an effort to create a work environment that is advantageous to our employees and to the company, we are designing a new concept of the employees' role in an industrial organization. The basis for this concept is rooted in our belief that each employee should get the following from their jobs: use their full capabilities; perform meaningful work; have the opportunity to advance on the basis of capabilities; be compensated on the basis of knowledge; and have the opportunity to control their work environment wherever possible.

We hope to accomplish these goals by the use of autonomous work teams. With the use of autonomous work groups, it is possible to integrate many different job assignments into one group and thus provide group members with an expanded work experience while providing the opportunity for employees to advance as rapidly as they can master new skills and differentiate pay only by the number of skills mastered. In addition, by setting the groups up around meaningful blocks of the manufacturing process, much of the decision making and control traditionally handled by foremen can be placed within the team for them to control within the group.

Figure 4.3, continued

The advantages to the company will result from decreased turnover and absenteeism, increased workforce utilization, and greater flexibility.

Source: Adapted from the company's statement of design objectives.

Plant Layout. In addition to the plant layout considerations specified in Figure 4.3, it seemed obvious to management that all the equipment under each team's control would have to be grouped together in one well-defined area. With this type of configuration, materials handling problems would be minimized and communications among team members would be facilitated.

The team concept influenced the plant layout in two other important ways. First, the plant was designed to make it easy for employees to meet in small groups. For this reason conference rooms were provided for use by the teams, and the lunchroom was located nearby to provide a convenient, quiet place for breaks. Management assumed that these informal gatherings would be an important source of job satisfaction for many workers, in addition to promoting intra-team and interteam work coordination. The second manifestation of the team concept was a deliberate effort to eliminate any status symbols that served to differentiate plant workers from office workers and management. To this end, the plant layout included a single, common entrance for plant and office, one lunchroom for all employees, an open parking lot with no reserved parking for management, and several points of access between the plant and office area.

Compensation System. The design objectives outlined in Figure 4.3 stated that the compensation system adopted should "differentiate pay only by the number of skills mastered." In effect, management made the decision to pay workers on the basis of what they knew rather than for what they actually did. Their reasoning was that workers who could perform many different tasks provided the company with more flexibility in their operations and could also serve as trainers of other employees, making them valuable to the company. Such a system also avoided the administrative problems involved in determining who did what job for how long — a potential nightmare in a system such as this one, which encouraged workers to perform all functions within their team's area of responsibility and to trade tasks regularly.

Management developed a five-level system for paying production employees. Each level of pay represented a different level of skill. The following general definitions of each pay level in terms of technical performance were agreed upon and used to develop specific technical skills standards for each of the teams. Levels 3-5 subsume mastery of the previous levels.

Level 1: Starting rate. New hire. Required completion of the introductory training course for basic skills in blueprint reading, gauging, and shop mathematics.

Level 2: Useful rate. Mastery of general, peripheral duties. Required to understand quality control procedures; able to set up and use gauges; capable of operating materials handling equipment; understands record keeping; familiar with and functional at housekeeping duties; familiar with all tooling and gauges, able to obtain these from the storeroom.

Level 3: Operator level. Able to operate all equipment within the team's area of responsibility, including making minor adjustments while the machinery is running.

Level 4: Operator setup level. Able to set up all machines and equipment in the team's area using prescribed setup procedures.

Level 5: Top team rate. Mastery of all team jobs and ability to serve as a training leader within the team. Able to troubleshoot machinery malfunctions, fully qualified to make mechanical repairs on team machinery, capable of administering preventive maintenance programs and of completing any outside courses deemed necessary.

In addition to their technical skills, each employee's team skills — that is, their ability to work together with other team members and to contribute to the effective functioning of the team — were to be evaluated as part of the process for determining pay increases. Instead of developing team skills standards for each pay level comparable to technical standards, the evaluation of team skills was to be done by the other members of the employee's team. If a team decided that a given employee's technical and team skills qualified him or her for a pay increase, they could recommend an increase to management. Management had initially decided that no employee would be considered for a pay increase unless recommended by the team. As these recommendations were filed, they could be acted upon in regularly held weekly meetings of the management team. Eventually, management expected to develop specific team skills standards for each pay level.

Management also decided that all production employees would be paid a monthly salary, instead of an hourly or daily wage rate. The monthly salary would cover a five-day, 40-hour workweek, and the salary system would be supplemented by extra pay for overtime, as required by the governing wage and hour laws. Also, a small premium would be paid for working on Sunday and for working on the evening and night shifts.

The salary system promised several advantages. One was that the status distinction between salaried personnel and hourly workers would be somewhat defused, an outcome consistent with the team concept. Another advantage of the new salary system was that it communicated management's belief that workers would act responsibly and not take advantage of a system wherein they would be paid for days absent. Another important advantage of the salary system was that it would do away with time clocks and the associated ritual of requiring workers to punch in and punch out every day.

Supervising the Teams. Plant G management did not wish to adopt the traditional system of having a supervisor for each work team. They were convinced that if the production teams had all the operating information and production plans usually possessed by a supervisor, individual operators could make the necessary decisions as well as a supervisor could — and that they could do it with less delay. Management also believed that increasing team members' decision-making responsibilities would serve to motivate the workers as well as promote job satisfaction.

At start-up, management instituted a system for supervising the teams in keeping with the team concept. The plan was to have two or three supervisors work each shift and be jointly responsible for supervising all the teams on that shift. Under this arrangement, no one supervisor would have direct authority over any one team and, presumably, the opportunities for production teams to manage their own affairs would be maximized. The plant manager described the management team's intentions as follows:

> We decided to start out without any direct supervision of these teams. We would have supervisors and they were going to be team coordinators

and resources for the teams. Some of them would provide a lot of technical assistance during start-up. We planned on having two of them on shift at all times. They had to cover seven days a week, so there were three per shift, and we had nine of those kind of people who were management's representatives. They were not going to function as foremen traditionally do. They might give orders to a team but they wouldn't say, "Ok, you go out and do this today." It's up to the team to decide who does what in order to get the work done. There's quite a distinction between our supervisors and the traditional role of foreman. They're going to operate pretty much as management's representative — but within the overall team concept.

The notion of having two to three supervisors sharing responsibility for a shift placed a great deal of strain on individual supervisors and served to cloud any notion individual supervisors might have had about their relationship to production teams. To remedy this situation, a series of meetings between the supervisors and the manufacturing manager was held in December 1975, in which it was decided to change the organization to one in which supervisors would be assigned to each of six production areas. It was hoped that this revised structure would allow supervisors to specialize in a limited set of production tasks and technologies. Under this structure some teams worked a different shift from that of the supervisor assigned to this area. The overall intent of the supervisory role remained unchanged, however.

Training and Development Program. Clearly, a substantial training effort was required. First, management knew that the area lacked a pool of trained machine operators. A basic machine shop skills program was needed, as well as specialized training with the types of machines to be used in the new plant. An equally important consideration was that most prospective employees required some training in the skills required to work effectively as members of a team. In a plant operating under the team concept, the workers' ability to function effectively as a unit and to maintain good work relationships was more important than in traditionally organized plants. Fortunately, Plant G had substantial resources available for the training program. As part of the resources provided by the state to attract new industry, the state provided a training facility near the plant, equipped the training center, developed a course in basic machine shop skills, and provided two full-time instructors. In addition, the state reimbursed Plant G for the salaries of three additional full-time National corporation employees (a training center director plus two instructors), trained these employees to be effective instructors, and paid the costs associated with securing the assistance of a training consultant from National's corporate employee relations staff.

The training program that emerged from the efforts of the project team was divided into two parts: a voluntary phase and a post-hiring phase. As discussed earlier, applicants were selected to undergo the voluntary phase of training, but they were neither paid nor promised a job unless they satisfactorily completed the voluntary training.

Phase I was designed to provide basic skills in four areas: technical skills, team skills, manufacturing process skills, and economic skills. Some of the materials were developed in a programmed learning format so that trainees could work at their own speed and at times convenient for them. Also, instructors for the technical and team skills training were available for morning, afternoon, and evening sessions so that trainees could hold their present jobs while completing the training program. All trainees who successfully completed the voluntary phase of training were then put on the payroll, to start phase II.

Phase II emphasized the development of a specific set of technical skills, depending on the team to which the employee was to be assigned at the plant; it provided additional training in team skills, process skills, and economic skills. Given that the plant had not yet started up when many employees were going through phase II, it continued to be held offsite at the training center. A major problem with the training was that while new hires were learning the basics of operating equipment similar to that found in the plant, they were unable to truly get exposed to the day-to-day routines and pressures they would face in the plant.

INTERNAL SOCIAL SYSTEM

The Supervisors' Role: Schedules and Organization

One supervisor discussed the situation on the floor before the move to organize supervisors around production processes:

It was a real zoo here after start-up. I'd come into work with no idea of what I had to do. We [the two shift managers] would just kind of roam around the floor checking attendance and monitoring performance. The employees didn't know who to come to for help and we were just as lost.

The intent of the change in supervisory organization was to provide for direct supervision of specific areas, as well as to allow for the development of technical expertise. The response to the change was generally positive except for one drawback identified by a number of supervisors:

The area-supervisor concept makes a lot of sense except for the fact that it has restricted my concern for the plant as a whole. I worry about what happens in my areas, with little concern for coordination with the other areas unless there is a really big problem.

Initially the area assignments were for single supervisors who were expected to manage areas across all three shifts. This allocation of duties did not work and convinced management of the need to add three additional supervisors.

In October 1976, an additional organizational change affecting the supervisory group was announced: the introduction of two unit managers into the organizational structure. As was mentioned earlier, each of these unit managers had six supervisors reporting to him and was responsible for overall coordination of a number of operating areas. Management presented three reasons for the introduction of unit managers.

Overload of the Manufacturing Manager. At the time of the change all the supervisors had reported directly to the manufacturing manager. The manufacturing manager was forced to be in the plant at all hours of the day and night and simply could not address the needs and questions of all the supervisors.

Perceived Poor Performance of the Supervisors. In the minds of the management staff, the earlier move to the area-supervisor concept had not resulted in satisfactory employee supervision and productivity. Members of management believed that more direct control of on-the-floor activities was necessary if production was ever to improve. An outgrowth of these feelings was the notion of adding another layer of management to work more closely with supervisors and teams.

The Need To Develop Enough Management Capability To Run a Seven-Day Operation. Several problems were identified as an out-growth of seven-day operations: lack of stability among work teams; increased absenteeism (laying out); reduction in shift supervision coverage; pressure on managers to remain close to the plant on week-ends; and inability to perform those duties on weekends that required support services, which worked a five-day schedule. One manager commented on the problem:

> We're trying to run a seven-day operation with five days' worth of managers. It's crazy. I bet that if we had started up as a five-day plant we would have the same total production as we've got now.

Administration of Rewards and Sanctions

A general feeling among supervisors was that they had little control over rewards and sanctions relative to employee behavior. Two particularly illustrative series of events frequently men-tioned by supervisors were the granting of pay increases to workers and the handling of absenteeism problems.

Pay Increases

When employees took the floor at start-up after completing the offsite phase II training program, most of the employees were rated as level 4 on the five-level scale. Management claimed this was done to show employees that there truly was going to be the capacity for advancement in pay. Some supervisors were con-cerned that this wholesale granting of pay increases represented a prostitution of the existing system. One supervisor commented:

> At start-up virtually everyone was a level 4 and virtually no one was really qualified for it. It set up totally unrealistic expectations of how the pay system was going to work and really bit us in the rear. When we confronted the management staff they replied, "We're expecting them to perform level 4 work and we're going to pay them for it."

In retrospect, members of the management staff believed they had mishandled the pay-increase issue; they recognized it as a factor that had contributed to increased employee turnover during the spring of 1976, the other key factor being that too many people were being expected to perform with inadequate training. One manager commented:

> People just didn't understand what we were doing and there were a lot of hard feelings about the way it was handled [the pay increases].

Absenteeism

Area teams and supervisors participated in a monthly responsibility allocation process designed to determine the functions to be assumed by the teams and supervisors, respectively. The process was not without its problems. One of the major problem areas revolved around the responsibility for handling absenteeism. A supervisor commented on the problem:

> My team tells me that they want to handle absenteeism. Then a vocal member of the group "lays out" and nothing is done about it. I speak with the team coordinator about the problem and he says he'll take care of it. Two days later he comes back and tells me that the team has decided I should handle the problem. This kind of thing happens all over the plant. When the team has to confront a strong personality they back off and throw the responsibility back to the supervisor. But if I went right out and confronted the worker myself the team would get all up in arms about management interference.

Supervisor Know-How

A review of the backgrounds of the Plant G supervisors indicates a clearly significant skills discrepancy. A number of supervisors who were hired before start-up made reference to the fact that they felt useless, as they had no background in ball bearings production technology, which meant they couldn't assist in new employee training, and had not gone through the employee training program. One of them commented:

> I was virtually useless during my first six months here. I was like a 300-pound high school coach trying to lead his team through calisthenics.

In concert with having a number of technically deficient supervisors at start-up, there was general agreement among management that they had overestimated the ability of the production teams to assume operating responsibilities. Consequently, these supervisors were unable to provide employees with strong leadership at start-up, with extremely disappointing results. One manager addressed the situation by commenting:

> What we needed at start-up were strong, technically oriented, production-minded foremen. Starting with an inadequately trained and poorly directed plant cost us dearly.

Those supervisors who had prior ball bearings manufacturing experience were generally respected by their teams for their technical competence. They were more likely than others to "get into" the equipment, and the teams appeared more willing to accept their technical assistance. By contrast, supervisors lacking the specific technical experience who attempted to intervene in technical problem-solving were often characterized as "interfering" with the team.

Beyond the general recognition of the start-up staffing error, there was very little agreement among the management staff and the supervisors on the role that supervisors were to play in the plant. Some viewed them as resources, facilitators, advisors, and consultants without any further specifics on what these functions entailed in terms of actual supervisory behavior. Others believed that the ultimate accountability for plant production fell on the supervisors. Some were totally unclear on just what the supervisors should do.

For example, a supervisor who had expressed great doubt that the team concept could work appeared to have one of the most highly developed teams in terms of productivity. At the same time, his teams were recognized as being extremely weak in terms of developing their social and team skills. They had no team meetings, no team skills training, and generally wanted explicit instructions as to what they were to do.

In the absence of an established core set of required skills for supervisors at Plant G, each supervisor molded the job to his or her own skills base. At the same time, the pressures of production, given the disappointing start-up, precluded providing attention to improving the skills of the supervisors through training. As one manager remarked:

We know that it's important and we'd like to train [supervisors] more than we do now; but the production pressure is so high we just can't afford to take the time.

Employee Expectations of Supervisor Behavior

Workers were especially sensitive to what they characterized as management interference by supervisors in their tasks. By management interference they were referring to what they considered unnecessary and unwanted supervisor involvement in what employees considered to be team activities. Two supervisors described their feelings about this problem as follows:

Sometimes when I go out on the floor, I feel like I have to tiptoe on eggshells. So, often I don't get involved with employees unless they specifically ask for my help.

I'm like one of those lizards that always change colors, except I don't have any control over what color I am. When the team wants me, I'm there. When they don't, I tread lightly.

Early in the plant's history, employees developed a tendency to bypass supervisors and to take up issues or concerns with plant management directly. This practice was partially explained by the minimal supervisor presence in the plant during its early months. Although managers indicated that the situation had improved it was still considered to be a problem. A manager remarked:

Sometimes we find ourselves stuck with problems that the supervisors should be solving with their teams.

Supervisors were particularly critical of situations in which they believed that workers had gone directly to the management staff with information critical to their performance.

Management's Expectations of Supervisor Behavior

It should not be surprising that our characterization of management's treatment of supervisors is one of erratic and inconsistent behavior. A number of possible explanations were available for the inconsistent behavior.

Lack of Agreement (Understanding) of the Intent of the Team Concept among Managers and Supervisors

It was apparent that management and supervisors viewed the rationale and intent of the plant design in different ways. Sample explanations of the rationale behind the team concept included:

This is the beginning of a social revolution.

You just can't manage people the way we used to.

We simply are interested in developing an organization that is more productive than our other plans. We're not interested in happy workers if they're not productive workers.

Efforts at clarifying the lack of agreement served to highlight the fact that people essentially had the same desired outcomes in mind but viewed their approaches to achieving them quite differently. At times, this lack of agreement manifested itself in mixed signals on implementation of action plans. As one manager remarked:

When one person says he did something after another person questions him on why it wasn't done, it often becomes apparent that they're just not talking about the same thing.

Pressure To Meet Production Goals

To some supervisors, the team concept meant that they were to be permissive. Increasing amounts of pressure to meet plant production goals found these supervisors reverting to behaving in more traditional ways. One supervisor commented:

The team concept is fine when we're producing. When we're not, things are the same here as they are every place else I've worked.

One manager believed that the management staff had recreated with supervisors many of the same problems supervisors were experiencing with their teams:

The supervisors will complain about something and we'll throw it back in their laps. They're afraid to come to us for guidance in developing a solution; thinking that somehow asking for assistance is a sign of weakness. Furthermore, they keep working issues among themselves thinking they have to come back to us with 100 percent agreement. By the time they finally come back to us, they're either too late or have neglected to consider one piece of information which we hadn't provided them. They really set themselves up to feel stupid and incompetent. Much the same kinds of things go on between the supervisor and his teams.

Supervisor Communications

Communications with Management

With the exception of the plant manager and the manufacturing manager, the management staff had no offices, maintaining work areas in an open office space instead. Given the seven-day work schedule, the open-plan office has enabled all managers present at any given time to be informed on a wide range of issues and to take action, even outside their functional areas, in the absence of other managers.

Although the managers believe they have sorted out responsibilities among themselves, this was not apparent to the supervisors – or if it was apparent, they appeared to ignore it. A supervisor who had a question could often be found going through the office asking the first manager in sight for an answer, regardless of whether it was the plant manager, the manufacturing manager, or a unit manager. An interesting cycle of events then fell into place. The supervisor would consider the first manager's answer inappropriate or hesitant and would then look for another manager to get a better answer to the same question. A supervisor often had to repeat this process two or three times before receiving a number of different answers, or a number of "I don't know – Go see Manager X," before reconciling the issue by saying, "Nobody here knows what the hell is going on. I'm not going to risk making a wrong decision, so I'll simply do nothing," or "Since nobody really knows the answer to my question, I'll wait until they tell me what to do."

This cycle was reinforced when managers continued to send supervisors to a manager who lacked the relevant information or decision-making authority and to attempt to pass on their "best guess" of the situation. This situation improved significantly with the introduction of unit managers, but it was still a problem in the opinion of many of those interviewed.

Communications with Peers

Supervisor/peer communications were generally described in positive terms. As one supervisor remarked, "We get along real well."

However, when probed, it appeared that there were significant problems in coordinating supervisory decisions. These problems generally cut across the supervisors on a particular shift. As one supervisor stated:

> With area management responsibilities, we just don't know what's going on in the rest of the plant unless someone tells us. And no one ever does until it's too late.

To ease difficulties in communications, the manufacturing manager began to hold supervisor update meetings during each shift. But despite the fact that they were perceived as useful, production pressures eventually intervened, and they had to be held only on a sporadic basis.

Communications with Hourly Employees

No formal communications vehicle was in place to provide for supervisor communications with hourly employees. For example, meetings could be called, but were not required. Furthermore, the performance level of team members was not evaluated on the basis of a formal system. As a result of these and many other factors, the behavior of the supervisors relative to the teams tended to vary significantly along several lines.

First, the tendency among supervisors to work to their strengths and to pay little attention to their weak areas resulted in different behavior. For example, a supervisor who had transferred from other plants would often be found with hands and head inside a piece of malfunctioning equipment, while a new supervisor would go around saying, "I'll never get inside a machine and tear it apart."

A second problem involved role-playing. In many situations supervisors recognized that the work team members possessed more knowledge about the equipment than they did. These supervisors tended to assume one or more of the following roles:

Go-fer: The teams used the supervisor as an errand boy.

Communications link: The supervisor spent large amounts of time transmitting information between various areas of the plant.

Team leader: The supervisor attempted to rely on interpersonal skills to get the team to perform to management's expectations.

Disciplinarian: The free time that resulted from an inability or unwillingness, or both, to get into the equipment, the supervisor often attempted to personally confront behavior he or she considered to be unacceptable.

Good guy: Another strategy was to attempt to motivate team performance by making workers feel indebted to Mr. Good Guy.

Third among the problem list was the real fear some supervisors had of "rocking the boat" by taking a strong stand on issues with team members. This appeared to lead to a number of behavioral outcomes that varied from issue to issue. For example, at times, some supervisors found themselves at the beck and call of the work team and did not attempt to influence the outcomes of team decision-making processes, even when they possessed additional information. At other times, some supervisors waited for declarative management directives before attempting to get their teams to implement any process or organizational changes.

A fourth problem, expressed by a group of supervisors, was a sense of frustration and impatience that grew out of their perception of the negative impacts of the team concept on production. The following behaviors appeared to be an outgrowth of these feelings: Depending on the circumstances, the supervisor would either listen to advice and/or directives from the management staff and then go out and then do his or her own thing; be less likely to hesitate to confront poor performers, inadequate mechanical troubleshooting, and so forth; or be more likely to violate a team's implicit norms of the team concept of operation.

Fifth, the move to the area-management concept reviewed earlier served to restrict the supervisor's concerns to a specific area of responsibility, leaving integration with other areas to occur only around crisis situations. This led to behavior that team members translated into the message, "as long as our production figures are good, why worry about the rest of the plant?"

Sixth, in the eyes of some team members, a number of individual supervisors displayed inconsistent behavior. There appeared to be a number of possible explanations for this perception:

Increased experience of supervisor: With experience, a supervisor might shift attitudes toward his or her role and relationships. These attitude shifts often exhibited themselves in ways viewed by others as inconsistent behavior.

Impact of mixed signals from management: The more members of the management staff a supervisor involved in making decisions, the more varied the data spectrum he or she was forced to cope with. The sheer magnitude of conflicting or inconsistent data presented to the supervisor appeared to result in inconsistent behavioral patterns.

Lack of feedback: The sole regular source of feedback that the supervisor could rely on was the daily production results. Beyond production results, feedback from superiors was irregular and generally negative in tone. The supervisor ended up with little feedback on past experiences to guide actions in present or future situations.

A seventh problem was a high level of paranoia. Lack of feedback combined with exclusion from a number of team activities has put a number of supervisors into a state of paranoia. When the only feedback supervisors received from management was generally negative and they were unable to find out what the team was doing, thinking, or saying in meetings, it was natural to assume that others were talking or complaining about them or their performance. Such feelings often led to erratic and inconsistent behavioral patterns.

Outcomes: Supervisory Satisfaction and Effectiveness

The disappointing production results of Plant G were compounded by similar disappointments expressed by a large segment of the plant population over the development of the supervisor's role. In three of the four formal skills areas in which supervisors were measured throughout the sample (people skills, organizational skills, technical and professional skills, and interdepartmental skills), Plant G's supervisors continually ranked lowest. They also ranked lowest of the four plants in overall supervisory effectiveness.

Given our description of Plant G and National Corporation's seeming inability to get the plant on track, these findings were not surprising. As supervisors continued to carry out an ill-defined role with little or no development or guidance, their behavior appeared increasingly inconsistent and erratic.

It was also not surprising that Plant G supervisors indicated the greatest dissatisfaction with their jobs among the supervisors in our sample.

FEEDBACK AND RENEWAL SYSTEMS

In our review of Plant G operations, we touched on the fact that supervisors lacked constructive feedback, attention, and contact on their performance. Outside of daily production results there were no standards for, or evaluations of, supervisory performance. The supervisory pay system at Plant G was essentially seniority based and paid little attention to reward for performance. No formal performance appraisal system was in operation.

The primary renewal system in evidence surfaced when supervisor discontent or frustration reached the point at which groups of supervisors vented on a manager or managers. While venting of frustrations has had some short-term benefits (and, in fact, did appear to lead to the move to an area-based organization for supervisors), it did not appear to foster an approach to identifying the problem, analyzing it, and then implementing a solution. For the most part, such sessions merely provided a simple emotional release.

A plantwide diagnosis was conducted by a team of corporate and outside resources in the summer of 1976. The management group appeared unable or unwilling to create a structure that would allow them to process the data collected and engage in action planning and implementation.

Although supervisors were continually reminded of the importance of their role in Plant G, they came to regard these reminders with increasing doubt and suspicion. One supervisor summarized the nature of the existing feedback and renewal systems when he stated:

> If we're so important here, how come no one has spent any time bothering to figure out just what we're supposed to be doing?

ANALYSIS OF THE SUPERVISORY SITUATION

Now to apply our conceptual framework to the supervisory situation as it exists at Plant G. As we outlined earlier, Plant G provided us with an opportunity to examine a supervisory workforce that appeared to be performing in a manner that disappointed all levels of the Plant G hierarchy and, when compared with other supervisors in our study, exhibited the greatest amount of job dissatisfaction. How can we explain these disappointing outcomes?

Start-up Relationships

Key Tasks and Technologies. Plant G was designed for the production of commercial-grade ball bearings, a task involving relatively complex machining skills.

Internal Social System. Management was committed to creating a productive plant through a team concept that would emphasize employee participation and self-direction.

Organizational Design. Management produced a comprehensive organizational design that supported the intent of the team concept.

Individual Characteristics of Human Resources. Management discovered that its design had dramatically overestimated the capacity of workers to master the technology and the production process. Most of the supervisors, being neophytes to the ball bearings industry, were of little help to their teams.

Organizational Outcomes. Production levels were disappointing. Workers, managers, and supervisors were experiencing considerable frustration with results.

Feedback and Renewal Systems. Pressures for daily production hampered the capacity of the plant management to collect, analyze, and use data regarding plant events. No formal problem-solving approaches were in place. Frustration led to emotional outbursts that stimulated band-aid changes — often with longer-term negative consequences.

Shakedown

Supervisor-Organizational Design

The Plant G organization provided us with a second example of an attempt at providing shop-floor employees with an attractive and challenging work environment that failed to take into account the supervisor's role. The initial design called for supervisors but for no direct supervision. Management then moved to area supervision and finally introduced unit managers as they increased the number of supervisors on the floor. At no time did management attempt to provide supervisors with a model for their activities; in fact, at times it appeared that they deliberately shied away from such action.

Also, given that the organizational design dramatically overestimated the capabilities of the workforce, no presence existed (short of the few experienced supervisors) to provide the technical leadership and support required for effective operation.

Lastly, given the absence of definitions of the supervisory role, little or no attention was paid to providing opportunities for supervisory training and development in an environment where worker training and development was a high-priority item.

The ambiguity of the supervisor's role and the lack of skills in role occupants combined with an increasingly frustrated workforce to raise constant cries of either a lack of support or supervisory interference. Relationships became strained.

Supervisor-Key Tasks and Technologies

A number of references have been made to the fact that the supervisory workforce generally possessed few of the technical skills necessary to be of assistance to work teams attempting to master the production process, as well as few of the skills necessary to assist a team in its social development. In other words, supervisors, not unlike the teams that reported to them, suffered from inadequate problem-solving, troubleshooting, interpersonal relations, and meetings skills, and were feeling increasingly insecure about their ability to develop in their teams' skills.

As a team's technical expertise increased through the experience of day-to-day operation, those supervisors who had a nontechnical background were being posed with what they perceived as an even greater threat — that of the team members being far more technically proficient than they and, as a result, reflecting on the supervisory presence as both unnecessary and unwelcome.

Supervisor-Internal Social System

The pressures associated with the disappointing Plant G start-up placed one clear message in the minds of most of the supervisors:

get production. Despite all the management energy and investment imbued in the team concept, it was clear that the plant manager, who played a key role in setting the tone or mood of the plant, was heavily influenced by day-to-day production results.

This push for production drove most supervisors to display a higher profile with their teams, a role that the teams were able to, and often did, reject. For example, supervisors were often excluded from team meetings. Lengthy team meetings would often interfere with critical production needs. Supervisors felt incapable of confronting the team over these issues. They began to view their role as having been emasculated by a lack of authority and began to miss the power and control they associated with a traditional conception of the supervisor's role.

They perceived a lack of support and direction from management. Managers provided supervisors with conflicting answers to the same issues. This confusion often served to immobilize the supervisors from action.

A vicious circle of activities in the supervisor-work team relationship was mirrored in the manager-supervisor relationship — one that the plant appeared incapable of arresting.

Key Tasks and Technologies-Organizational Design

Continual reference has been made to the fact that the design created by the Plant G management underestimated the complexity of the machining technology given the employee population. Nowhere was this more evident than in the employee training program. The expectation of the training program design was that people could transfer the machining skills learned offsite to different equipment in the plant with the additional burden of production pressures. It clearly was not the case.

Key Tasks and Technologies-Internal Social System

The significant gaps in skills among supervisors and work teams to handle the demands of the technology contributed greatly to Plant G's disappointing results.

Organizational Design-Internal Social System

The development of a work team's ability to increase its self-management capabilities appeared to be inconsistent throughout the plant. The design was vague as to just what supervisors were to do to assist their teams to become a self-managing unit. A typical statement from a confused supervisor characterized the problem:

> My teams are all different. For example, this week all of my teams had meetings to discuss the steering committee activities. One took a half-hour to do it, one took one and one-half hours, and the third team took two hours — all with the same proposed agenda. And since I wasn't allowed to sit in on the meetings, I couldn't be of any help to them. If this is the team concept, I'm not so sure it's worth the effort.

With managers skirting the pay issue and some employees viewing supervisors as hiding behind the team concept, the freedom with which segments of the organizational design were violated began to shake the credibility of the concept in toto. It became increasingly legitimate for supervisors to raise concerns with the concept in general.

SUMMARY

National Corporation's Plant G suffered greatly from poor implementation of many of the design characteristics that had been skillfully laid out on paper. As a result, no clear-cut plantwide picture emerged as to the extent of employee participation. Participation levels varied greatly from team to team and from shift to shift.

Plant G management failed to prepare employees, supervisors, and even themselves for the implications of the course they had chosen for their operations. Skills levels were low, and little was done to raise them. Management responses were generally one-shot attempts that lacked lasting impact. It was not surprising to find that Plant G suffered from the poorest overall performance record of the sites studied.

Most supervisors in Plant G carved out their own individual roles, hence there was little consistency in role definition. With management attention focused on improving results over the short term, this situation was permitted to stand.

In addition, as was true for Plant O, many of the gains in quality of work life at the team-member level appear to have been matched with a corresponding decrease in the quality of work life for supervisors.

A simple commitment to making some plantwide decisions regarding the supervisory role and the monitoring of supervisory behavior against the decisions that have been made would go a long way toward restoring some sense of sanity in the supervisor's work life.

NOTE

1. Portions of this section have been adapted from Robert W. Le Duc, "The Plant Y Project (A) & (B)" (Boston: Harvard Business School Case Services, 1977).

5

Case Study: Plant J

OVERVIEW OF THE PLANT

Plant J was one of five domestic manufacturing plants of Anderson Motors, a major producer of diesel engines and components, with operations located in North and South America and Europe.* The plant began operations in early 1976 in a facility purchased two years earlier from the Gem Steel Products Company, which had moved its production facilities to a new location.

Plant J was located in a heavily Scandinavian community in the Northeast. The economy of the local community had suffered severe declines during the early 1970s, as much of the local industry had shut down operations and had moved to other areas in which the costs of operation were perceived to be lower; other firms simply went out of business. Many of these relocations appeared to be related to a poor labor relations climate that had

---

*All identifications relating to the plant and to the company have been disguised.

plagued the community with frequent shutdowns and strikes. Through the direct intervention of the local government, many of the remaining employers and labor unions had joined together to establish an areawide labor-management task force in an attempt to improve the base level of labor-management relations in the community. The committee has met with some success in accomplishing its mission and has fostered the establishment of a number of joint labor-management quality of work life projects.

During its search for a plant site, which began in late 1973, the management of Anderson Motors was offered a large facility, suitable for its operations, at an extremely attractive price. In spite of all the problems outlined in the plant J community, Anderson Motors elected to establish its plant in that town.

The company informed the local political and industrial leaders that its plans called for eventually hiring 2,000 persons at Plant J, which would provide quite a boon to the local economy. The company also stated its intentions, despite the unionized status of most of its domestic manufacturing facilities, to start up as a nonunion facility. It was assured by local labor leaders that it would be allowed a reasonable period of time at start-up without immediate threat of an organizing drive.

At the time of this study (August 1977), the plant employed approximately 470 people in a variety of operations that ran either one, two, or three shifts on a five- or seven-day basis. Expectations for full employment at Plant J, heavily dependent on the general economy and on Anderson Motors' markets, would not be reached before 1982-1983.

INTEREST IN CREATING A PARTICIPATIVE WORK SYSTEM

Plant J was the second new plant in the company to explore and implement an innovative, highly participative organizational design. A team of managers and internal and external behavioral science researchers spent several months conducting site visits at other companies, exploring the available literature on quality of work life, and organizing their knowledge within a framework compatible with the manufacture of engine components. In addition, the earlier new plant had met with a rocky start-up, and managers had directed much of their effort avoiding the problems encountered in their plant.

From April through December 1974, the managers and resources established a set of guiding principles and an operating mission statement, an organizational structure and principles for the design of jobs, and a framework of supporting systems (which Plant J labels as plant practices), all in anticipation of a productive start-up in 1975. The national economic recession of 1974-1975 had a significant impact on the engine business; it forced Anderson Motors to make the decision to delay production at Plant J for an additional year. This would give managers and other personnel already on board in 1975 additional time and energy to develop the plant practices further and to identify the characteristics of a Plant J operating style.

An internal document used for employee training, permitted start-up managers to voice their interest in creating an innovative organization (Fig. 5.1).

KEY TASKS AND TECHNOLOGIES

The key tasks and technologies of Plant J can be divided into two distinct categories: components machining, and engine assembly and testing.

At start-up, Plant J was designed to operate strictly as an engine components machining operation that would support the requirements of the engine assembly and testing operations located at other facilities and the engine aftermarket. In mid-1976, a shift in corporate strategy added the assembly and testing of a model line of diesel engines to the plant's original responsibilities. Planning was initiated immediately, with an interim engine assembly and testing operation beginning production in the late spring of 1977.

Components Machining

At the time of our study, the plant was involved in the manufacture of four components: a camfollower/cambox, an air compressor crank case, a piston, and a flywheel. Plans called for the plant to assume responsibility, over the next two to three years, for the manufacture of five additional components, with the potential for several more in the years after that. Each of these operations was both equipment and materials intensive. Generally, the plant used the most advanced proven manufacturing technology, including the

FIGURE 5.1
Plant J: A Different Organizational Style — Why?

Our work system is showing symptoms of imperfection:

- Worker dissatisfaction and alienation — absenteeism, turnover, strikes, sabotage, poor quality, and noncommitment
- Reduced worker productivity
- Increased emphasis on quality of life-leisure, social benefits

These symptoms are interpreted many ways. Many agree that:

- Work changes have not kept pace with worker competency, values, and social systems.
- Meaningless repetitive tasks without learning and growth have turned-off the creative abilities of workers.

A new plant start-up provided the opportunity to reassess and revise our methods of organization and management by considering changes in the meaning of work to:

- Reverse the decline in employee productivity.
- Reinforce high expectations and accomplishments.
- Minimize meaningless dissatisfaction.
- Develop and use employee creative abilities.
- Provide motivating influences, including self-managing work teams, whole tasks, and flexible assignments for career development.

Source: Internal company document.

use of robots equipped to perform a number of routine dull tasks generally performed by human beings, in a few operations. In addition, the cost of raw materials factored significantly into the ultimate plant cost of a component. For example, the raw materials cost for a finished piston comprised approximately 65 to 70 percent of the final product cost. The total cost of direct labor represented approximately 4 to 7 percent of the final product cost.

The machining equipment was generally highly complex, requiring continuous monitoring and maintenance. Final product specifications were often strict and required production to relatively exacting tolerances. Consequently, not identifying a problem early in a production run or not monitoring the quality of machined products coming off the equipment could easily result in the required reworking or scrapping of large numbers of components.

The production needs and staffing levels of the various component manufacturing areas (each area being under a single supervisor) gave each a great deal of flexibility in determining the number of shifts and days worked. The result of this flexibility was the lack of a consistent work schedule throughout the plant.

Engine Assembly and Testing

Plant plans called for the eventual production of 300 engines per day (by 1983) evenly distributed across two independent assembly lines. As mentioned earlier, at the time of our study, production was taking place in an interim assembly operation that bore little resemblance to what the ultimate operation was expected to look like.

The primary purpose of the interim operation was to begin to expose plant employees to the basics of engine assembly and test operations through a hands-on, self-paced operation. An additional purpose of the preliminary assembly operation was to encourage informed employee input into the final assembly design. The major outcome for the assembly area at the time of the study was not production — which was artificially being restricted to eight engines per day — but quality. If Plant J could develop the capacity to build a high-quality engine requiring little or no rework or repair before shipment, enormous cost savings could be generated (the assembly operation being considerably more labor intensive than the components-machining operation).

INDIVIDUAL CHARACTERISTICS OF HUMAN RESOURCES

Supervisors

The demographics of the supervisory workforce are outlined in Table 5.1.

Given the relative newness of the facility, it was interesting to note that six of the nine supervisors were promoted to their position from hourly work teams. The high percentage of team

TABLE 5.1
Composition of Plant J Supervisory Force

Employee	Sex	Age	Time As Supervisor in Plant J (in years)	Previous Supervisory Experience (in years)	College
1[a]	M	27	1	None	None
2	F	26	1	1	B.S., Engineering
3[a]	M	35	1	10	None
4[a]	M	28	1/2	None	None
5	M	35	1-1/2	5	B.S., Industrial Administration
6[a]	F	32	1/4	None	Some courses
7[b]	M	38	1-1/2	6	None
8[a]	M	27	1/3	None	Electronics school
9[a]	M	28	1/2	None	None

[a]Promoted from hourly workforce.
[b]Supervisory transfer from another Anderson Motors plant.

114

member supervisors created some interesting dynamics in the plant, which we shall explore in greater depth later. Only four of the nine supervisors possessed any previous supervisory experience or post-high school training, and only one supervisor had transferred to Plant J from another Anderson manufacturing facility.

Plant J managers attempted to tap a number of sources for supervisory positions, recognizing that this was a uniquely demanding role to fill, given their mode of operation. Examples of these efforts included the recruitment of recent MBA and college graduates, supervisors from other Anderson plants, and supervisors from competitors' manufacturing facilities. For a variety of reasons, these efforts were largely ineffective, resulting in the workforce outlined above.

In order to guide the Plant J managers' efforts in the process of selecting supervisors, the plant manager of organizational development prepared a role description that was believed to describe the requirements of this nebulous role, outlined in the following description from an internal company document.[1]

The Plant J. Supervisor's Role

General Description
A supervisor means many things to many people. The intention of this memo is to serve as a guide to the selection and training of supervisors. The elements of a supervisor's role are sorted into the categories of interpersonal skill, technical skill, and growth.

Interpersonal Skill
- *Understands and effectively practices an effective* style of communications *including listening to others in a way that makes them feel comfortable in expressing ideas, speaking clearly, concisely, and to the point of discussion, helping others to express their ideas, testing assumptions, and guiding group and individual decision making.*
- *Capable of a* flexibility of style *as is appropriate to various situations. Knowing when to be participative vs. directive, how to deal with groups and individuals. Guiding direction, measuring results, and giving feedback.*

- Problem solving *processes: Works to bring conflicts into the open, helping to resolve conflicts as appropriate, able to take independent stands, raise and help resolve issues and represent issues with subordinates, peers, and superiors. Integrating and promoting direct communications, keeping an open door and an open ear to all issues. Able to understand and take into consideration the motives and interests of others. Balance the needs of consensus and decisiveness.*

- Leadership: *Setting objectives, results measurement in ways which are seen as objective, understandable, and fair. Coordination training resources, directing others towards self-sufficiency, aggressiveness in pursuing objective initiative, planning, and implementation of plans. Delegate to others in a way which consistently tests and develops their skills, competency, accountability and responsibility for the accomplishment of objectives. Maintain an orientation towards the accomplishment of all goals and commitments, with an effective sense of pace, timing, and priorities. Maintains systems discipline, including the ability to understand and explain why a given system is in place, and the self-discipline to avoid the violation or working around existing systems for reasons of short term expediency, and holding others accountable for maintaining the same standards of discipline in their actions. Maintains adequate pace and level of achievement.*

- Inspires the confidence, *respect, and trust of others through actions characterized by effective listening, maturity in maintaining confidence and confidentiality of information that allows an effective meeting of the counselor role. As appropriate, refers persons to other resources for assistance.*

Technical Skill
- *Some interest and/or experience in one or more of the following areas of technical skill which are utilized in the machining of diesel engine components and in the assembly and testing of diesel engines, and in all associated support activities:*
  - *Machining: Operate, setup, routine maintenance, diagnosis, repair, design, and so forth.*
  - *Assembly/Test: Schedule, perform, trouble shoot, repair, inspect, and so forth.*
  - *Purchasing: Order via set purchase order, vendor contact, receiving inspector, vendor development, and so forth.*

- *Materials: Movement, Inventory system, scheduling, heat treat, and so forth.*
- *Quality: Following and maintaining set inspection procedures, deviation requests, laboratory work, and so forth.*
- *Accounting: In-process inventory, scheduling, shipments, develop production accounting, provide training in accounting, and so forth.*
- *Engineering: Mechanical, electrical, production, manufacturing, product, industrial, metallurgical, and so forth.*
- *Personnel/organizational development: Selection, orientation, training, counseling, compensation, labor relations, affirmative action.*

The depth of knowledge required in each of these skill areas will vary in different situations and with different teams. The key is an ability and interest to quickly understand enough of what is affecting a team's operations in a given situation to help that team effectively deal with the situation. The supervisor may either directly input information or know very quickly where and how to get appropriate resources. The supervisor's effectiveness rests in being able to quickly understand situations and to facilitate resolution.

Growth

- *Feeling comfortable with the idea of succeeding only through the efforts of others with the success of the team being the prime measure of the success of the supervisor. Feeling secure in delegating responsibility and accountability to others without having the need to second guess, look over their shoulders or take control. Give others the chance to succeed and to make mistakes and learn from those mistakes.*
- *Sense the correct rate of change as a team and individual team members mature, and allow increasing self-sufficiency.*
- *Mechanically inclined: At least curious enough to learn about machinery and assembly and be as familiar as becomes appropriate to serve to identify the need for other resources and to provide some training in some situations. Establish a fundamental credibility with the team through the demonstration of willingness to roll up the sleeves and get your hands dirty, avoiding any pretense of superiority.*
- *Capable and interested in quickly learning in every circumstance that presents itself, and taking pleasure in presenting that learning to others.*

• *Business sense: Has a healthy, competitive spirit and willing to generate the energy to meet a difficult goal, be self-confident, and decisive, be well organized setting priorities and following through on those priorities.*

• *Sees a value in volunteering and spontaneously getting involved in the multitude of opportunities which occur.*

• *Maturity: Self-confident; doesn't succeed at subordinate's expense, respect and basically trust the motives of others, self-motivated and self-starting, demonstrating initiative, functioning well with ambiguity and willing to act without precise directions or clear precedent.*

• *Able to handle pressure and willing to make special sacrifices, especially sacrifices of time. Tolerant in frustrating circumstances with ability to think through, and help others think through, difficult situations and circumstances. Avoid blaming others, in situations where attributing blame is not likely to see positive end result. Not a quitter.*

Workers

All applicants for work at the Plant J start-up were subjected to participation in three distinct interviews. The first was designed to assess the skills and capabilities of the job candidate and was generally conducted by a member of the personnel department. The personnel department then selected a second interviewer, generally a line manager, to conduct an interview designed to address an applicant's interest in personal growth and learning. The job application was constructed to provide the candidate with opportunities to address these issues in writing. Lastly, the applicant was provided with a third interview directed at explaining the compensation and benefit system.

Soon after completing the interview, the interviewers would meet to discuss and evaluate the information obtained from the candidate and prepare a ranking. The personnel department would then collect and compare the results from all the current applicants and make hiring decisions.

This system changed dramatically after start-up. Workers were provided with interview training and were qualified to participate in the screening interviews and selection process. Personnel played a prescreening role and would forward applications to a work team with a job opening. The qualified members of the team and, generally, the supervisor then conducted group interviews for a select number of candidates and made the ultimate hiring decision, which was passed on to the personnel department for implementation.

Both selection processes were designed to assist in staffing up Plant J with employees eager for challenge and flexibility in their work; for the most part, the processes served the plant well.

Nevertheless, the selection methods did not yield a typical Plant J worker in evidence throughout the plant. There was a wide range of ages and educational backgrounds. Women were well represented in the workforce, and minorities were represented in proportions exceeding the community average (still they are a rather small percentage). The most pervasive descriptive characteristics were employees' general willingness to be vocal in expressing their feelings and needs, and so forth, as well as their commitment to working hard to meet the goals they set.

Managers

In staffing the management positions at Plant J, a deliberate emphasis was placed on finding employees considered capable of, and interested in, the challenges of the broadened job responsibilities and innovative management structure outlined in the next section.

As a result of this emphasis, Plant J was staffed with a large number of managers who had developed better-than-average track records in previous assignments. They were generally quite aggressive and career oriented. None assumed a position in Plant J with responsibilities beneath the level of the previous position, although from a corporate standpoint the move to Plant J might be considered a lateral one.

The plant manager, as we shall highlight later, played a key role in the plant, shaped in large part by his outgoing personality and his willingness to verbalize his feelings to people at all levels of the organization.

ORGANIZATIONAL DESIGN

Structure

Critical to the understanding of Plant J operations is a thorough exposure to its structure, one that was unparalleled within Anderson Motors.

At the top of the organization was a plant manager, who held ultimate responsibility for overall plant performance. Reporting to the plant manager were five directors, a materials manager, and an organizational development consultant. This group comprised what was called the plant operating team. They were responsible for the overall coordination of plantwide policy and direction.

Four of the five directors (as can be seen in Fig. 5.2) functioned at the head of one or more staff and line manufacturing operations. For example, the director of personnel headed up the administrative office operations as well as manufacturing operations for three components with their corresponding support functions. The intent of combining line and staff responsibilities under a single manager was to minimize the traditional infighting between operating and support groups.

The unusual amount of responsibility and opportunity in the directors' positions was thought to serve a significant inducement for managers to move from other Anderson facilities to Plant J.

Reporting to the directors were a complement of functional and business managers. The functional organizations were thinly staffed and held responsibility for the development and coordination of plantwide policies and systems as well as reporting and audit procedures carried out in the six individual businesses. The business concept represented the plant's desire to provide for decision making to take place as close to the shop floor as possible. It also represented an attempt to avoid the problems experienced by managers associated with large manufacturing facilities through the establishment of a number of miniplants, each of which would eventually be staffed with 150 to 200 people. Each business had its own manufacturing operations as well as engineering services, maintenance trainers (called skills trainers at Plant J), materials coordination, financial, and general training functions.

Each of these businesses was headed up by a business manager, who, like the directors, was provided with unparalleled responsibility

FIGURE 5.2
Plant J: Organization Chart

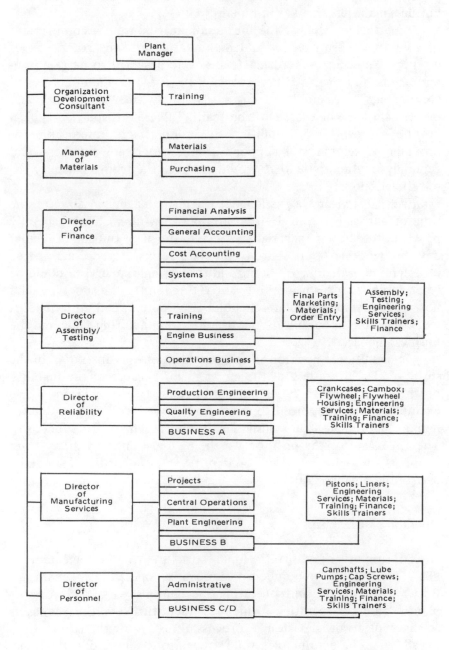

at his or her level within the Anderson organization. In essence, business managers acted as miniplant managers.

Reporting to each of the business managers were a complement of two to five supervisors and manufacturing teams composed of workers. These manufacturing teams were designed to be as autonomous as practical with responsibility for the manufacture of components or assembly of engines. As many tasks as possible and practicable were delegated to the team. Table 5.2 displays a typical outline of team responsibilities. Supervisors were responsible for providing developmental support, training for team members, and generally anything else that would enhance the team's capacity for self-direction.

Each supervisor was assigned to a team ranging in size (at the time of our study) from six to more than 75 workers. They generally provided the only managerial presence in the plant outside of regular daytime working hours. Given that their teams played a major role in determining their work hours and that a single supervisor could be responsible for a team working across three shifts, the supervisor did not work a stable, regular schedule. Each determined an individual work schedule in consultation with the manufacturing team and the business manager.

One additional position in the organization was instituted in the spring of 1977 in a few of the larger teams because of the inability of the supervisors to cover all shifts. Called shift advisors, these exempt positions reported to the supervisor and were responsible for helping coordinate team activities in the absence of a supervisor. The necessity for the position was being questioned by many team members, and the position could not yet be identified as a fixed part of the organization.

Operating Mechanisms

To support the organizational structure, the management of Plant J developed a number of innovative operating mechanisms. Both the structure and operating mechanisms were built on the plant's guiding operating principles identified by the managers at the outset of the design process: trust, growth, equity, and excellence. These principles translated into a set of organizational goals and characteristics that guided their design choices, as

TABLE 5.2
Plant J: Manufacturing Team Responsibilities

Job skills
    Operations: Machining/assembly

Operate/assemble/test	Maintain production records
Set-up	Tool sharpening/control
Change tools	Maintain necessary supplies
Maintenance	Specifications interpretation
Inspection/process control	Rework/repair

    Quality assurance

Maintain gauges/tools	Documentation
Inspect purchased material	Supplier/customer contact
Audit finished materials	Final inspection

    Packaging
        Shipping
        Machine runoff
        Cost control
    Material handling
        Vehicle operation
        Minor vehicle maintenance
        Documentation
    Planning/scheduling

Delivery goals	Inventory control (raw, in
Machine loading	process, finished)
Scheduling	Contact with customers

    Documentation

Budgeting	Cost records
Production records	Attendance/payroll records

    Team administration

Overtime	Attendance
Shift assignment	Interteam coordination

Team responsibilities

Goal setting	Documentation
Goal attainment	Cost reduction
Team member selection	Communications
Team member training/orientation	Performance measurement
Housekeeping	Compliance with "expected
Safety practices	behaviors"

Source: Employee orientation manual.

outlined in the following description from the employee orientation manual.[2]

Plant J Goals

- *Produce a quality product, on time, at the lowest possible cost.*
- *Provide a mature working environment where the worth of an individual is recognized and employees are encouraged to contribute up to their capability.*

Plant J Characteristics

- *Recognition of individual worth/talent/desires and structure work and rewards accordingly*
- *Cooperative teamwork at all levels, with many tasks designed for team achievement requiring cooperative relationships*
- *Opportunities for individual growth within equivalent skills levels and advancement to higher skills levels, with growth, learning, and development recognized and rewarded*
- *Clear accountability and responsibility for the achievement of specific goals and objectives cooperatively arrived at; responsibility to be placed at the action level, with goals integrated for machine, man, and organization*
- *Participative decision making at all levels regarding elements which affect each person's work environment. Participation implies disciplined involvement and not a personal choice to pursue an independent objective.*
- *Recognition of achievements — continuous challenge*
- *Encouragement of innovation, risk taking, and change*
- *Provision of flexibility and versatility*
- *Development of trust at all levels*
- *Simplified compensation and benefits system which minimizes status differentials (nonexempt vs. exempt) but does reward on the basis of skill development achievements, flexibility, and level of responsibility.*
- *Minimal status differentiation*
- *Simplicity in organizational design without excessive rigidity in structure*

• *Provision of open communications and feedback at all levels — plant, production, and company matters*
• *Socially satisfying*
• *Excellence expected*
• *Jobs designed to perform whole tasks where possible and permit all positions to plan, do, control*

The key design operating mechanisms are outlined as follows.

Hourly Employee Salary System. The hourly employee salary system was rooted in four key principles:

1. Reward achievement on skills acquisition rather than solely on length of service.
2. Encourage employee and team growth and development.
3. Recognize past experience.
4. Develop team and plant flexibility.

The system was based on five salary or skills levels that team members were expected to advance through over approximately five years. It was designed to allow the peak salary to be achieved without a worker changing teams under the presumption that the teams were correspondingly designed to contain at least five meaningful growth modules and that job rotation and training and teaching of job skills were legitimate uses of team members' time. The development and acquisition of skills were measured through the developmental review process outlined below.

Workers were paid a salary, rather than hourly wages, on a biweekly basis. The intent of Plant J management was to maintain salary levels competitive with the top industrial wage rates in the community.

Developmental Review System. Performance of all employees was to be measured and evaluated by their superior through the developmental review system. The review process contained sections on self-directed development, development planning, self-evaluations of performance, and consensus as to the next steps. It was designed as the integrating component for the salary system, organizational design, and goal-setting system and was designed initially to be conducted on a quarterly basis.

Board of Representatives. Rooted in the belief that all employees should have the opportunity to participate in establishing and maintaining plantwide policies and practices that affected their working environment, a board of representatives was composed of persons selected from business, functional, and support teams. The objective of the board was to establish and administer, as well as review, policies regarding plantwide responsibilities delegated to them by the plant operating team, such as: cafeteria; plantwide charitable contributions; recreation; parking; and plant practices, including problem-solving, corrective action (discipline), reassignment/transfer, expectations, communications, attendance, working hours, layoffs, overtime, safety, security, loan out, and parking.

Task Descriptions. A major focus of the design effort was to define the range of the various team responsibilities through detailed team, rather than individual, task descriptions. These served as the basis for measuring and evaluating performance.

Discipline. The designers of Plant J rejected a traditional discipline system in favor of one that emphasized constructive counseling for corrective action. Employees were considered capable of correcting unacceptable behavior once it was understood. After a number of infractions, the corrective action system called for employees to be sent home, with pay, to assess the appropriateness of their continued employment at Plant J. Such employees were then expected to return to work prepared to inform their team and/or supervisor of what they would do to express their continued desire to work at the plant. Only after repeated demonstrations of unacceptable conduct and unwillingness to correct behavior would an employee be terminated.

Orientation. An intensive two-month orientation program was coordinated with the on-the-job training gained on the work team. This orientation program was designed to expose new workers to the rationale behind the Plant J system and to the expectations of employees at Plant J as well as to a basic knowledge of the engine business and Plant J operations.

Cost System. Given the significance attached to employee self-direction, it was believed imperative that employees have a strong basic knowledge of the economics of their operations. Standard cost accounting reporting systems were considered wholly inadequate in that regard, in addition to being far too complex. Plant J management set out to provide workers with a simple, yet comprehensive, cost system and designed a system on the basis of cost per piece (e.g., component, engine) that highlighted the economic impact of controllable (variable) and noncontrollable (fixed) costs associated with final product cost. This system also served as the base for a cost-reduction program emphasizing net reductions in cost per piece.

Issues Task Forces. A variety of plantwide groups, in addition to the board of representatives, existed for employees to raise and work issues. Examples of these groups included the affirmative action task force, the nonexempt compensation task force, skills trainers issues task force, and support managers group.

Lastly, in highlighting the organizational design, it is important to note that Plant J managers saw it as one that would be constantly adapting and evolving as new issues were raised in association with the continuing growth of the organization. There was explicit recognition of the fact that the design that worked for a plant of 470 employees would not work for a plant of 2,000 and that continual attention needed to be paid to fine-tuning and changing the organization. An additional group called the operations review group (ORG) was charged with the responsibility of diagnosing problems and making recommendations on many of the major design issues not covered by other issue groups.

INTERNAL SOCIAL SYSTEM

Supervisor Know-How

Plant J relied, for the most part, on promotions from the nonexempt employee ranks to supervisory positions. Although they often represented the height of technical competence within the plant, these employees certainly were not able to develop the technical expertise that comes from spending years around an engine-building plant. Supervisors recognized their lack of expertise and thought improvements would occur as time passed. Business managers, on the other hand, appeared quite a bit more apprehensive about the lack of experienced supervisors on the floor.

Plant J's business managers indicated a desire to achieve a mix of supervisors on the floor — some with BAs, some with MBAs, older people with lots of engine experience, and others upgraded from the Plant J nonexempt ranks. During the course of our study, however, a number of the managers appeared to have given up on these ideas as being unrealistic. As one business manager put it:

> I've been trying to fill a number of supervisor positions for quite a while. I've gotten no response from our other plants and had exceptional difficulty interesting anyone from the outside in the job. Outsiders relate to salary grades and titles. Here, they get neither and are turned off.

And as a director stated:

> What we want just doesn't exist. If we find someone with technical skills, he generally has very little in the way of interpersonal skills, and we really need people with a balance of skills for a supervisory position.

The strong reliance on in-plant promotions and the apparently unsuccessful attempts at recruiting supervisors to Plant J fostered the belief among much of the hourly workforce that supervisory jobs should be filled only from within. The guiding principle of growth began to take on the meaning of promotion to team members. Major concerns were expressed by managers that (1) the expectations of advancement held by the hourly workforce were unrealistic and could lead to strong disappointments; and (2) if they were able to bring in outside supervisors, they might have problems dealing with a large number of team members who viewed them as an outsider who had stolen a promotional opportunity for themselves.

Team members were able to develop skills in many operating areas at rates that negated any potential technological superiority on the part of the supervisor. As one supervisor remarked: "My team members are equal to me or above me in technical skills." This fact led some supervisors to pay a great deal of attention to continuing in technical training programs.

Supervisor Responsibility and Accountability

It is in this area that we see the substantial impact of the Plant J mode of operation. Most of the supervisors who were interviewed accepted a great deal of personal responsibility for what they viewed as probably the most significant task associated with their role, namely, developing the team to be self-managing while maintaining good day-to-day performance.

At the same time, there was some confusion over the ways in which supervisors should carry out their role relative to the work teams. A supervisor stated:

> Feeling unclear [about one's job] is pretty common around here because there are no operating guidelines.

But at this early stage of the plant's history, and with the relative newness of many of the supervisors, this situation was not at all surprising. In fact, a supervisor summed it up as follows:

> We have so little history that the fact that I don't really know what my responsibilities are is not surprising. We define our jobs as we go along. When I first became a supervisor this bothered me quite a bit, but it doesn't anymore.

Another potential explanation for the confusion lies in the general lack of performance feedback that reached the supervisor. Again, the newness of many supervisors contributed to this situation. More than half the supervisors who were interviewed stated that they had little or no idea as to how their performance was being viewed by their business manager. This insufficient feedback often resulted in supervisors defining their roles and determining areas of responsibility with the assistance of whatever feedback they received — generally from team members. The conclusions reached by supervisors did not necessarily match the expectations of their business manager.

Despite all the innovations in Plant J that appeared to call out for a new role for the supervisor, they often found themselves infused with a traditional (nonparticipative) production mentality. Given the lack of feedback from business managers and the fact that daily production statistics provided concrete, timely feedback, it was not surprising to find supervisors who managed for "the numbers." A problem resulting from this tendency was that lateness or absence from meetings, complaints about paperwork, and missed project deadlines were not uncommon experiences with the Plant J supervisor. A business manager highlighted the problem as follows:

With many of the supervisors "production is King" and everything else is peripheral. I'm the one who pushes my supervisors to do the other tasks (other than production) and I haven't got the time to monitor them that closely.

Another explanation for the apparent time-management problem was that many of the skills necessary for efficient and effective overall performance were not yet developed in the supervisory or employee workforce. For example, a supervisor remarked:

I spend almost 50 percent of my time in meetings where we keep kicking around problems but seem to accomplish very little. I haven't got the time to run my area and go to all the meetings.

While a business manager commented:

All the questioning that goes on here forces us to have lots of meetings. But we don't know how to run them very well. People are beginning to back off and keep quiet to avoid sitting in hours of unproductive meetings. We have to find some way of avoiding this.

Given the intent of the Plant J design, it is also appropriate to assess work team performance in the context of their willingness to accept responsibility. Supervisors expressed considerable pleasure with the way in which most of the teams were "picking up the ball and running with it." They remarked quite favorably on the sense of responsibility they believed their teams showed. However, four of the supervisors interviewed said that, in spite of their overall positive feelings, there appeared to be abuses of the system by team members. A sample of the remarks included:

You don't call in sick in another plant if you've got a headache. You might here.

The responsibility felt by team members for their own areas and, to a lesser extent, for the plant as a whole contributed to a healthy questioning of policies and actions. It was not at all uncommon for team members to push for clear justifications of management or supervisory actions. This placed pressure on supervisors to develop a number of coping strategies:

First, supervisors themselves had to be well informed and pushed to obtain clear justifications from their superiors so that they could keep people informed. One supervisor highlighted this issue:

> Even when the team members were new and supervisors by necessity were a lot more directive, I always made sure to be able to explain to people why we were going to do something.

Second, supervisors pushed the teams to make as many decisions as possible, thus avoiding, whenever possible, having to defend their actions. As a supervisor remarked:

> Almost everything I do gets bounced back to the team. I might direct them early on by voicing my opinion but I really push them to accept responsibility for developing the ultimate policies and procedures, rather than question those that I would otherwise develop.

In terms of individual team members accepting personal responsibility, there inevitably were a number of problem employees who required supervisory presence of a disciplinary (corrective action) nature. Supervisors expressed general displeasure or dissatisfaction with their role in the process:

> It really bothers me to give corrective action and I'm not having much success with it. Many of the team members I've worked with have been defensive to feedback or have withdrawn from counseling. It is clearly the most distasteful part of my job.

However, there was recognition that the Plant J design, the employees selected to work in the plant, and the corrective action program contributed to a smaller number of problems reaching the supervisor than one normally would find in a traditional plant. A supervisor with experience in both traditional and innovative systems commented as follows:

> Corrective action rather than discipline has fostered an increased tendency for people to police themselves and apply peer pressure. I'm doing a lot less performance counseling here than I ever did in prior jobs.

Supervisor Communications

Communications with Management

Supervisors generally reported communication with superiors in a positive tone. The positive aspects stressed by supervisors were its informality, the lack of paper communications, and the emphasis on face-to-face conversations which encouraged supervisors to raise issues. Some representative positive comments included:

> I feel really comfortable with my boss. We can discuss team problems and he's always quite helpful. He doesn't push answers on me but allows me to think things through.

> I can always go directly to the manager who has the information I need to get without having to get my boss's permission first.

Two supervisors working for the same business manager expressed disappointment in the amount of one-way information transfer that took place with their superiors, complaining that meetings with their boss were usually one-way communications.

Communications with Team Members

Supervisors recognized the importance of building strong interpersonal relationships between themselves and their teams, as well as among team members. Supervisors and team members took part in communications and human relations sessions as part of their training, a practice that was perceived as useful.

Team meetings were held at the start of each shift. Lasting from 15 minutes to more than an hour, the meeting was generally used for the supervisor and team members to review the previous day's results, to share any relevant information with the team, to plan out the day's activities in detail, and to do longer-range planning when it was called for. The meeting also often became a forum for airing problems widely shared by team members and for attempting to resolve them. Supervisors maintained that the major value of the team meeting lay in its role of helping build closer relationships among team members and with the supervisor.

Supervisors, as a group, had a positive attitude about the quality of communications with team members. Communications problems with team members were most prevalent with newer supervisors who were attempting to reduce their profile with the younger teams:

> I often have difficulty in getting them to really open up and blast me if I'm doing something wrong. That's probably because I began by being directive with them.

Communications with Peers

Of all the directions of supervisor communications, the least satisfaction appeared to be derived from peer interactions, as is highlighted by their comments below:

> We'll interact around production and personnel and that's about it. It's been kind of a letdown.

> When there were just a few of us, things were super; as soon as the group grew we had to fight like hell to keep together.

In addition the problems associated with the increased number of supervisors, many of the problems appeared to be rooted in a number of strongly held feelings among the upgraded supervisors, developed about one another when they were team members. One supervisor commented on the problem:

> Not everybody likes everyone else. There are strongly held opinions that some supervisors are not very competent. As a consequence, sometimes people end up not being interested in what others have to say about anything.

The communications problems, in conjunction with a number of other factors, contributed to the difficulties experienced in getting supervisors together for training meetings:

> Some supervisors turn those meetings into little more than bitch sessions. That's not a very good use of my time.

Communications among supervisors within the individual businesses was recognized as being much better than those on a plant-wide basis.

Motivation and the Supervisor

The design for Plant J rested on a fundamental notion that people wanted to do a good job and built in a number of support mechanisms on the basis of that key assumption. Supervisors were continually encouraged by management to provide additional responsibilities and challenges to the team members. A number of supervisors expressed surprise as to the extent to which people wanted to assume additional responsibilities:

> I rapidly found out that team members could do much more than I originally thought, so I could be much less directive than I thought I needed to be.

> My team continually sets production goals that are higher than what I came in with, and they really are motivated to stick to theirs.

Problems arose when some of the operating mechanisms intended to provide team members with a stimulating and motivating environment seemed to interfere with a productive environment in the short run. These problems were most prevalent in the areas of acquiring additional skills for promotion, and in aspirations for promotion, as evidenced by such supervisory comments as:

> We were faced with a situation where team members focused in on their developmental plans and rotating assignments and avoided doing many things which needed to get done. We needed to get some specialization and have people spend more time on machines than it takes to be barely trained. So I had to make an unpopular decision to assign personnel to machines and tell the team that's the way it was going to be whether they liked it or not.

> One of the big problems here is that people equate growth with promotion to supervisor. If we promote everyone, we'll never have anyone to run the machines. But we can't discourage people for trying to become exempt.

Supervisors routinely worked long hours and weekends without additional compensation. Although it was generally unnecessary, one could generally find a supervisor in the area when a team had to work extra time or weekends. One supervisor commented:

Very few of us want to work weekends and I don't want to expect any team to do things that I wouldn't do. So when they work, I work.

Supervisor as Trainer and Developer

Trainer

The unique organization of Plant J had a heavy impact on the way in which a supervisor fulfilled the training role because most supervisors lacked the technical skills to the same degree as their team members and consequently could not be of much assistance in training others; the plant had a training support function that tended to fulfill this role; and in attempting to get teams self-managing, it was viewed as a team function to train new team members.

In terms of their role as technical trainer, the early supervisors tended to play a high-profile role in training team members as well as in learning other areas alongside their teams. The supervisors' role in technical training had decreased to the point where most supervisors spent virtually no time doing technical training.

By contrast, supervisors viewed their role as social skills trainers to be a critical one. They indicated that they spent considerable time helping the team develop and improve its capacities for problem solving and conflict resolution.

Developer

A number of formal mechanisms (e.g., developmental reviews, corrective action) were in place to be utilized as vehicles for supervisors to assist in employee and team development. While team development appeared to be progressing satisfactorily, individual development activities were not being carried out as well, especially with regard to performance feedback. This situation could be attributed, to a large extent, to the fact that supervisors have not received performance feedback. A director summed up the situation with the following comment:

I think we're all committed to the concept of developmental reviews. We just don't do them.

Supervisor as Planner

Most of the planning observed at Plant J was of a short-term nature, and interviews did not yield a picture of supervisors engaged in long-term planning processes, other than one supervisor who spent a large portion of her daily schedule working on a large-scale project.

A few of the supervisors indicated the desire to get involved in project work, yet recognized that their current workload made it impossible to be involved in a project with fixed deadlines:

> I had a lot of free time for a while. So I asked for some project work. As soon as I started work on the project the team needed more of my time. So I was forced to drop the whole idea. As soon as we have stable experienced teams, I'll be able to get back to it.

As most of the supervisors were new to their positions, they expressed a real need to spend additional time in their position learning the ropes, in sharpening their interpersonal skills, and in experiencing more of what it was to be a first-line manager before moving on to longer-term projects or a new assignment.

In fact, some of the supervisors expressed the belief that more of the planning responsibility currently was in their laps than they cared to have. One supervisor remarked:

> If we [his department] sneeze, the company coughs. We've already put another plant on half-speed for two days. Given the importance of the situation, I'm always changing plans and schedules to meet immediate needs. It's just too much for one person to handle on top of all the other responsibilities we have.

ORGANIZATIONAL OUTCOMES: SUPERVISORY SATISFACTION AND EFFECTIVENESS

As a group, the supervisors in Plant J were perceived as generally being moderately effective. They ranked as the third most effective supervisory workforce in our sample of plants (behind Plants O and F). They ranked in the midrange of our sample in the evaluations of a variety of supervisory skills.

Given the newness of most of the supervisory force and the ambiguity surrounding their role, these results were quite complementary to the supervisory group.

At the same time, Plant J's supervisors evidenced much greater job satisfaction than did their counterparts at Plants O and G. Only Plant F's supervisors indicated greater job satisfaction than Plant J's. The same results surface when analyzing supervisors' attitudes toward plant leadership. Once again, only Plant F's supervisors held more positive feelings about the top management of the plant.

FEEDBACK AND RENEWAL SYSTEMS

We have reviewed numerous mechanisms in place at Plant J that were intended to promote the surfacing and resolution of problems and issues. It is interesting to note that, at the time of our study, no vehicle existed for working concerns shared by supervisors.

Attempts at getting supervisors together as a total group were meeting with some resistance for a variety of reasons:

1. The animosity among some supervisors
2. The number of meetings supervisors were already attending
3. The press of short-term production needs

However, supervisors did meet on a business-wide basis, and in conjunction with the business manager, did appear to be able to address some common issues on a limited scale.

ANALYSIS OF THE SUPERVISORY SITUATION

In this section we shall attempt to analyze the supervisory situation in Plant J through the use of the conceptual framework introduced in Chapter 3. Plant J's supervisory workforce was generally viewed as effective and indicated relatively high levels of job satisfaction, when considered in the context of our sample of plants.

Start-up Relationships

Key Tasks and Technologies. Plant J was designed for the machining of diesel engine components, using state-of-the-art technology.

The manufacturing process required a variety of manual, inspection, maintenance, and administrative skills.

Internal Social System. Management was committed to developing an effective operation through high levels of employee participation and self-direction.

Organizational Design. A comprehensive organizational design was implemented which supported the objective of employee participation and effective operation. The design restructured traditional jobs at all levels of the organization — not just at the worker level.

Individual Characteristics of Human Resources. The worker selection system was highly effective in providing a workforce whose backgrounds, attitudes, and values were compatible with plant needs. Managers from other facilities were attracted to unparalleled career opportunities for them at Plant J. Attempts at recruiting and selecting supervisors for the plant ran into great difficulties. Most of the supervisors were promoted from the hourly workforce. They were not only new to the engine business; many had no previous supervisory experience.

Organizational Outcomes. Not surprisingly, supervisors experienced frustration with the ambiguity of their role. Over time they were able to recognize that their role was inherently ambiguous, and frustration levels dropped considerably. Teams were generally developing at an impressive rate and production and costs were encouraging.

Feedback and Renewal Systems. With the recognition that the plant would experience significant growth over the next decade, and with the knowledge that organizations must be constantly adapting and changing, a large number of mechanisms were in place in the plant for data gathering and continual fine-tuning of the organization. No such system, however, was in place specifically to address supervisors' needs and problems.

Shakedown

Supervisor-Organizational Design

The Plant J organizational design effort can be clearly differentiated from those in Plants O and G in that it paid attention to the design of jobs at the managerial level, as well as on the shop floor. There was explicit recognition that quality of work life was for everybody in the plant. In the context of the design effort, Plant J was the only plant in the sample that put into writing a descriptive statement regarding the nature of the supervisory role and attempted to use the description in the recruitment and selection process.

However, it is clear that significantly more attention was paid to the manager and team member roles. From reading their supervisory role description, one concludes that the traditional man-in-the-middle label for supervisors seems tame, given the expectations held for Plant J supervisors.

With the skills that were identified as being necessary for the Plant J supervisory role, it was surprising that the plant, after experiencing some initial difficulties, almost totally backed away from going outside for supervisors and promoted from within. Initially, many of these selections appeared to create numerous problems and frustrations in supervisors and workers alike. As one director stated:

> Most of the supervisors we have are new to that kind of position and appear confused and fairly jealous of the responsibilities they are willing to share or delegate, especially those things they perceive as positives for them. It appears that what we need in the supervisory role are people who have done all these things before and who have no hang-up about delegating them.

It appeared that, with the passage of time, the teams and supervisors were, in most cases, able to work out relationships which became increasingly satisfying and effective for them.

Supervisor-Key Tasks and Technologies

We have made numerous references to the fact that although, early on, supervisors often represented the height of technical competence in the manufacturing areas, they were, in fact, lacking in relevant previous experience. For the most part, they possessed few of the technical skills to be of significant assistance to the teams in their attempts to master the technology. However, the plant possessed a training function as well as skills trainers positions, which effectively supported the supervisor. As teams gained in their ability they increasingly assumed the bulk of the responsibility for training new team members.

The major problem associated with a technically weak supervisory force was their general inability, at start-up, to be of significant assistance in technical troubleshooting or problem solving on the production floor during operation.

Supervisors have, for the most part, quickly learned, and been able to effectively delegate to their teams, many of the nontechnical support functions required to be carried out in each area.

Supervisor-Internal Social System

As time passed, as relationships were built, and as people's basic competencies were enhanced, there appeared to be an increasing congruence in the supervisor-team relationship. Interestingly, the major misfits appeared to occur in the relationships between the supervisor and the business manager. The business managers were generally so busy trying to accommodate themselves to the demands of a dramatically expanded role that they were experiencing significant difficulties in fulfilling their traditional coaching and development role with supervisors. During the early stages of their supervisory assignment, virtually all the supervisors received little or no feedback from business managers.

This lack of feedback clearly was a major factor fueling the early supervisory frustrations. It also tended to push supervisors toward managing for production results (the only clear unequivocal feedback they received), sometimes in ways conflicting with team growth and development.

Key Tasks and Technologies-Organizational Design

The organizational design of Plant J was unusually comprehensive relative to the key tasks and technologies. The emphasis on team task descriptions, rather than on individual job designs, and the development of the capacity for self-direction in no way conflicted with the demands of the technology.

The growth and development (skills-related) promotion modules built into the pay system, the development track for team members, and the availability of skills trainers and other technical support at start-up were all congruent with the demands of a plant start-up and its ongoing operations.

As was highlighted earlier, the major problem with the fit between design and technology lay in management's failure to recruit a cadre of technically proficient supervisors.

Key Tasks and Technologies-Internal Social System

The relationships between supervisors and work teams appeared to contribute to task accomplishment in an efficient and effective manner today. Much of the normal rockiness of a plant start-up was no longer observable, and each successive new manufacturing area appeared to be started up more smoothly, given a base of experienced team members to assist in the operation.

Organizational Design-Internal Social System

For the most part, the guiding principles of the organization design appeared to be carried out on a day-to-day basis in the plant.

The major problem area that had potential impacts for the supervisor was in the expectations for personal growth held by team members. If the perception that all available supervisory positions be filled by team members persisted, there would either be a disappointed and angry workforce and/or problems with the introduction of new supervisors from the outside.

One of the most significant strengths of the design lies in the explicit recognition that the organization, as it grew, was in a transitionary state and its organizational design must be both adaptable and flexible. None of the elements appeared to be in a state that would inhibit the flexibility of the organization to make appropriate fine-tuning changes for the supervisory role if they were called for.

SUMMARY

The management of Anderson Motor's Plant J attempted to develop a highly participative work system that called for significant employee involvement in most plantwide issues and virtually all work-related systems.

They adopted a number of innovative structural and design characteristics to assist them in their efforts: the business team concept, the developmental review system, and the board of representatives being among them. And actual participation levels in many facets of the business were high.

Plant J attempted to develop a general description of the supervisory role, an attempt unmatched by the other sites we have studied. However, despite this description, there was significant role confusion at start-up along with high levels of supervisor frustration. This was not surprising. The confusion lessened somewhat over time, and frustration levels dropped dramatically as supervisors came to recognize and accept the ambiguity inherent in the role.

This initial confusion could be traced to a number of factors; not the least being that the role defies simple description. While the management did a thorough job of designing the plant, they, along with the new supervisors, were suffering from the ambiguity inherent in the newly created roles of business manager and director. Their natural tendency when confused, uncertain, or overloaded was to gravitate toward traditional behavioral patterns, hence the lack of developmental feedback provided to supervisors. This lack of feedback added to the confusion inherent in an already dynamic situation.

Team members, on the other hand, appeared clearer on the implications of the system for them and were constantly observed pushing for additional responsibilities and decision-making authority. The supervisors' early perceptions that managers were looking for the bottom line, given the absence of any other feedback, more than team development, and that team members were looking for additional authority, had resulted in a great deal of stress during the early months of a supervisory assignment. This stress had to be confronted and worked through with both managers and team members should the supervisor successfully continue in the assigned position.

The plant's bottom-line results to date have been highly satisfactory, and the president of Anderson Motors has been extremely impressed with the plant. But as the plant, and consequently, the teams, increase in size, the supervisory role will continually have to be fine tuned. Mechanisms to assist in this process need to be developed and instituted in the plant.

NOTES

1. Internal company document, 1977.
2. Employee orientation manual, 1976.

6

Case Study: Plant F

OVERVIEW OF THE PLANT

Plant F was one of four battery manufacturing plants that comprised the Automotive Electrical Supply Division of the Federal Products Corporation, a major multinational corporation with interests in the transportation industry.* The plant was started up in fall 1974 to produce the newly introduced "maintenance-free" automobile battery — a battery that was sealed during the production process and that required no upkeep from its owner. The plant was brought onstream with the intention of having it service a significant portion of the forecasted demand for this new product.

Plant F was located in a small southern town of approximately 10,000 people. The nearest major metropolitan area was more than 200 miles away. It represented the only significant industry in the immediate area. Although the town fathers welcomed the arrival

---

*All identifications relating to the plant and to the company have been disguised.

143

143

of Plant F, they were concerned about the possible effects of the wage scale they would be offering. With the nearest domestic multi-plant employer located 60 miles away, the town employment was based in farming and the fiber and leather industries, each of which employed approximately 400 persons. It was feared that if Federal Products were to adopt a wage policy in Plant F similar to those maintained in its northern plants (Plant F was started as a nonunion organization), the disruption to the community's economy would be enormous. These concerns were dispelled by Plant F's commitment to maintain a maximum workforce of approximately 350 persons and by the knowledge that the small plant size, combined with Federal Products' relatively stable employment policy, would minimize any potential impact on the community. Another major concern of the community was the potential of unionization at Plant F, given that all the other plants in the division were organized. The town leaders were quite adamant about their desire not to have unions in the community, because of their potential spinoff effects on other employers and on the farming industry.

At the time of this study (November 1977), the plant employed approximately 350 people distributed across a two-shift/five-day operation.

INTEREST IN CREATING A PARTICIPATIVE WORK SYSTEM

Plant F was the first new plant in the division to design an operation that applied the knowledge available at that time on employee productivity and the quality of work life. The plant manager had retreated to an offsite facility with his six key reports several months before start-up to design the operating system with the assistance of consulting resources from the corporate organizational development department. Much of the interest in adopting a new organizational form for Plant F was rooted in the desire of the plant manager to create a working environment that would be more satisfying and productive than the strongly unionized and highly rigid environments common throughout the rest of the division and to which he had most recently been exposed in his prior job assignment.

In addition, the start-up management team at Plant F received a great deal of encouragement and support from the corporate consultants. Segments of corporate management were vitally interested in having "quality of work life" projects begun in a variety of different settings at Federal Products: old and new plants, different divisions, and unionized and nonunion locations. They viewed the start-up of Plant F as a unique opportunity whereby entry into a division could be gained.

KEY TASKS AND TECHNOLOGIES

The basic steps involved in the manufacturing of maintenance-free batteries can be summarized in Figure 6.1.

The process of battery manufacturing, from a direct labor standpoint, was not terribly complex. Most of the production functions required manual dexterity in the sense of basic hand assembly skills.

The unique aspect of the task and technologies of Plant F lay in the newness of both. The plant was designed to produce a new (never before manufactured in volume quantities) version of maintenance-free batteries and used the most sophisticated state-of-the-art technology. Much of the production equipment, in fact, had never been tested in a Federal Products plant under operating conditions. We will explore the significant implications of this management choice later in the case.

The battery covers and cases were, whenever possible, produced and stored for later use. Virtually all other elements of the process were designed to operate with little or no work in process inventory. A glance at the flow diagram of the production process shows the obvious major interdependencies among the steps of the production process, as well as the fact that production difficulties at virtually any step of the process had the capacity to shut down the entire manufacturing process once the limited work in process was worked through the plant. As a result, the manufacturing process called for a high degree of coordination among the various operations.

It was also imperative that the production process be continually monitored and evaluated. Simple errors in the production process, if not discovered and corrected, had the capacity to render large quantities of finished product useless. And although the tolerances that employees of Plant F worked to were not nearly as exact as those of ball bearings manufacturing at Plant G or components

FIGURE 6.1
Basic Steps in Manufacturing Maintenance-Free Batteries

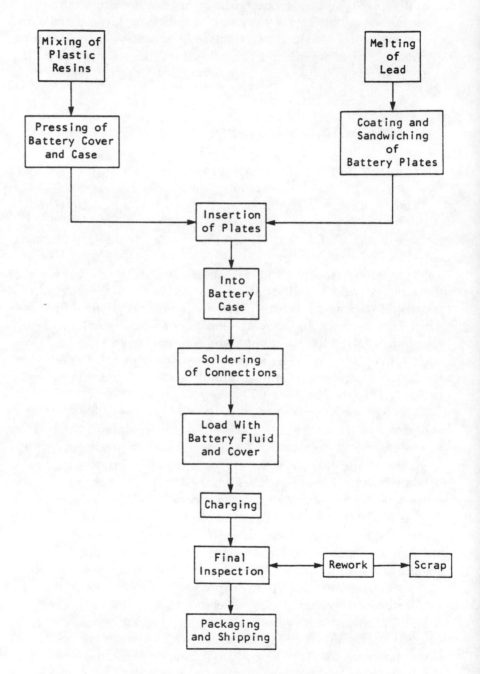

machining at Plant J, they nevertheless required a high degree of attention to detail.

INDIVIDUAL CHARACTERISTICS OF HUMAN RESOURCES

Supervisors

The supervisory workforce was divided into five areas of responsibility: production, maintenance, shipping and receiving, technical services, and quality control. Table 6.1 presents an overview of the composition of this group.

Of the 12 supervisors at Plant F, eight were promoted to their position from the hourly or clerical workforce at the plant. Six of the supervisors possessed previous supervisory experience, and three had training beyond high school. Two areas (technical services and shipping and receiving) were fully staffed with transfers from other Federal Products plants who have been in their positions since the plant start-up. In the production area, however, all four supervisors were promoted from the hourly workforce and, although three possessed previous supervisory experience, they were in industries totally unrelated to battery manufacturing.

As can be seen from Table 6.1, the production supervisors have been in their positions for only 1½ years. During the first year of operation, Plant F maintained no direct employee supervision in manufacturing areas. To place other sections of this case into context, we will review a bit of the plant's history of operation at start-up. relative to the supervisor's role. At start-up the plant had five supervisors (one in maintenance, three in technical services, one in shipping and receiving), all of whom had transferred from other Federal locations. The demands of the start-up stretched these five supervisors, as well as the management of the plant, to their limits. The new technology required greater technical resources present than Plant F had. Consequently, equipment troubleshooting and debugging were taking place but were very slow. Division headquarters loaned Plant F upward of 60 engineers who worked around the clock to get the plant up and running. At the same time, manufacturing personnel in division headquarters issued an edict to install direct employee supervision in the plant. The tone of the message bore the implication that this was not to be a negotiable item, and the plant responded by promoting four production supervisors from the floor. Manage-

TABLE 6.1
Composition of Plant F Supervisory Force

Employee	Area	Sex	Age	Time as Supervisor (years)	Previous Supervisory Experience (years)	College
1[a]	Production	M	31	½	None	A.A., Accounting
2[a]	Production	M	31	1½	8	None
3[a]	Production	M	31	1½	13	None
4[a]	Production	M	31	1½	2	None
5[a]	Maintenance	M	34	1	1½	None
6[b]	Maintenance	M	27	2½	2	B.S., Electrical Engineering
7[b]	Technical services	M	32	2½	2	B.S. Chemical Engineering
8[b]	Technical services	M	35	2½	None	None
9[b]	Technical services	M	48	2½	None	None
10[a]	Quality control	M	29	2	None	None
11[a]	Quality control	M	34	2	None	None
12[b]	Shipping and receiving	M	36	2½	None	None

[a]Promoted from hourly or clerical workforce.
[b]Transfer from other Federal Products plant.

ment indicated that the decision to promote from the floor was made on the basis of three criteria:

1. The need was to satisfy process demands unique to the plant; production supervisors from other plants would not know the technology.
2. They had been borrowing supervisory resources from division headquarters who functioned at Plant F as technical resources. Given these employees' frustrations in helping to get the plant started up, their desire to transfer to Plant F was not great.
3. The plant's greatest needs were in planning and coordination, and they thought they had internal people who could fill those roles.

Workers

The hiring practices of Plant F represented a management commitment to affirmative action goals, which called for the plant workforce to be representative of the community labor force. Fifty percent of the employees were black and 25 percent were women.

The most consistent description for the workforce was that they were "green but enthusiastic." For approximately 75 percent of the workers, their job at Plant F would be their first exposure to a manufacturing operation of any kind. However, one could sense the excitement among most of the workforce, even after 2½ years, about working in Plant F.

Also, at the plant start-up, the average per-capita family income in the local community was approximately $3,800 per year. Employees at Plant F would start out (with no overtime) at approximately $8,500 per year. A job at Plant F was a "rare plum" and people took great pride in being selected to work there.

Plant F departed significantly from established corporate practices in the recruitment and selection of hourly employees. Applicants for positions at Plant F made their initial contact with the plant through the State Employment Agency. The state conducted an initial rough-cut prescreening of applications and referred the bulk of the applications to the plant. The plant personnel manager selected those applications that he felt exhibited promise and invited applicants in for initial interviews with one of the managers on the start-up team. At this point in the process, two-thirds of the applicants were screened out. The next phase of the employment process employed a group assessment center with 12 applicants and two to three managers, later to include additional operating team members as the plant came onstream. The assessments consisted of five one-hour exercises designed to display an applicant's communications and teamwork skills. Approximately 50 percent of the candidates assessed were rejected from further consideration. The intent of this process was to get people who not only could express their own thoughts and feelings, but could and would listen to others.

The remaining candidates were invited to participate in the Plant F Rapid Start program, a 31-hour prehire training program in product familiarization, safety, first aid, communications and group problem solving, and basic plant economics. Virtually all employees who began the Rapid Start program successfully completed it and became regular employees. All this prescreening was conducted on the applicants' own time.

Managers

As we mentioned earlier, the plant manager at Plant F was quite enthusiastic about the potential to create a more satisfying and productive work environment than had ever been seen in the division. He did not want to be the plant manager of a new plant that would rapidly assume many of the dysfunctional characteristics of the facility he had recently transferred from.

All six managers he chose to help him design and start-up Plant F were selected for either their perceived compatibility with, or sympathy for, the ideas the plant manager held for Plant F. They were, for the most part, a young group of managers, all of whom accepted promotions to come to Plant F. And each held career aspirations that went beyond Plant F.

ORGANIZATIONAL DESIGN

Structure

The Automotive Electrical Supply Division was a major supplier of electrical components for Federal Products, as well as a significant participant in the replacement parts market. The growth of the division directly paralleled the growth of Federal Products in their markets.

Federal was long recognized as a highly effective and profitable corporation. It maintained an aggressive management-recruiting organization that, in combination with the Federal Institute, a cooperative educational facility authorized to grant university degrees, supplied much of their lower level manufacturing manager needs. The first-line supervisor's job was not considered a managerial position and recruiting at this level throughout the division generally was directed at the higher-quality hourly employees. The various divisions maintained presupervisory screening training and 12-week supervisors' schools.

Plant F operated under the structure outlined in Figure 6.2. At the top of the Plant F organization was the plant manager who held responsibility for the total operation of the plant, served as the representative of the company to the community, and provided the key interface with corporate management. A plant superintendent reported to the plant manager and had responsibility for all production, maintenance, and technical service personnel in the plant. He also served as acting plant manager in the plant manager's absence. This position served as the key training spot for potential plant managers. The next level of managers consisted of those responsible for the functional areas of maintenance and technical services, production engineering, purchasing, personnel, and quality control. The plant superintendent and the maintenance and technical services, purchasing and quality control managers each had from one to four supervisors reporting to them. It was these individuals (and most particularly production, shipping and receiving, and maintenance supervisors) who maintained direct interface with the work teams and were the primary focus of our study of Plant F.

The four direct area production supervisors each supervised 50 to 75 employees divided into three to six work teams that ran different portions of the production process. Each of the maintenance supervisors supervised 10 to 12 general maintenance personnel while the quality control supervisors directly coordinated a small lab staff. The shipping and receiving supervisor had a team of 18 employees across two shifts.

Production requirements, product specifications, and marketing plans were developed at division headquarters and implemented through consultation with the plant. Plant F was an organization dedicated to servicing the in-process product requirements of other

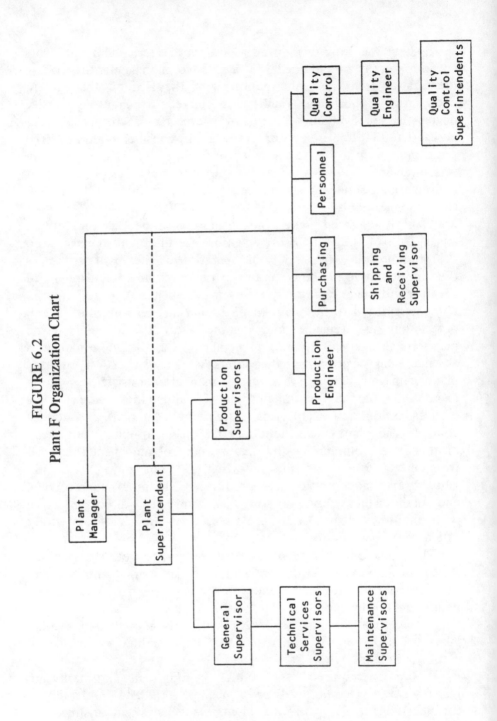

FIGURE 6.2
Plant F Organization Chart

divisions of Federal. They were expected to go to great lengths to meet the demands placed on them by others in Federal.

Operating Mechanisms

The Support Team Concept and the Plant Philosophy and Goals

While the corporation was conducting the last stage of the search for a new plant site, the seven members of the new plant management team engaged in a process of deciding how the plant should operate and what improvements in their management techniques could be made to minimize the dysfunctional aspects of their currently operating plants. They initially determined a set of behaviors to operate under as a management team[1] :

1) We will work for consensus on decisions, objectives, and plans.

2) We will share openly and authentically with others regarding our feelings, opinions, thoughts, and perceptions about problems and conditions.

3) When listening, we will attempt to hear and interpret communications from the sender's point of view.

4) We will trust, support, and have genuine concern for other team members.

5) We will respect and be tolerant of individual differences.

6) We will utilize the resources of other team members.

7) We will encourage comments on our own behavior.

8) We will understand and commit ourselves to team objectives.

9) We will not engage in win/lose activities with other team members.

10) We know that integrity of line authority must be maintained to keep an effective team.

They then moved from issues of their own functioning as a management organization (which they renamed the Plant Support Team in an attempt to signal their interest in minimized status distinctions in the plant) to issues of the plant as a whole. The process began with the drafting of a plant philosophy and goal statement, which served as the base for the organization design. These statements appear as Figures 6.3 and 6.4, respectively.[2,3]

In connection with these statements, the support team adopted a plant motto of "people helping people" that they hoped would stand as a key component of employee and managerial behavior.

FIGURE 6.3
Plant F Philosophy

It is our objective to have the most efficient plant possible. We will do this by combining the technical and human resources of our plant through a participative management style. That is, every employee at Plant F will share in the managing of the plant.

We want all employees to participate because:

- The way our plant is managed will affect the behavior and performance of all employees.
- Every individual is unique and can contribute to the success of our plant.
- People are more responsible when given responsibility.
- People support what they help to create.

We believe that continuing research and change is necessary for this continuing success of our business.

We believe that by organizing our work in a way that will fulfill the personal needs for self-respect and personal improvement, we will help achieve an efficient plant. Because we are all working toward the same goal of an efficient Plant F, we must all work as a team. Cooperation is more effective than competition.

They decided that they wanted to have an organization that was highly communicative in nature. They believed that if they could bring onboard a group of people who could communicate both effectively and openly, both vertically and horizontally, the personnel problems that plagued other plants would be minimized. Furthermore, they expected that production process difficulties could be dealt with more expeditiously and that a general spirit of cooperation and unification could be developed to improve both the quality of the product and the quality of work life. Second, they decided that they wanted to install a team concept of operation, modeled after many of the successful ongoing projects at other companies they had heard about. They decided to start-up the plant with three kinds of teams: operating teams, technical service teams, and the support team.

FIGURE 6.4
Plant F Goals

The goal of the Plant F Team is to be a successful organization. We can improve productivity by utilizing people's minds, as well as their hands. Additional goals are directed towards satisfying the needs of those affected by our operations:

- Our employees
- Our customers
- The community
- Local, state, and federal government
- Our stockholders

Through the effective use of human, financial, and material resources available to us, we will work towards the following:

- To produce a defect-free battery in high volume while staying responsive to changing market needs
- To upgrade the quality of work life by providing a safe, steady, and meaningful employment to our work force
- To encourage involvement and participation by our employees in an atmosphere of trust, communication, and opportunity
- To be an active citizen of our town and the surrounding area and to do our share to promote the growth and prosperity of our community
- To follow policies that will comply with equal employment opportunity, environmental requirements
- To contribute to the profitability and return on the investment of our Division of the Federal Products Corporation and our stockholders

---

The plant operating teams were composed of manufacturing and assembly personnel who would be performing regular production type duties. The technical service (maintenance) teams would do the complicated skilled maintenance type work, and the support teams (the top levels of management) would provide the resources for the other teams in areas such as reliability and quality control, purchasing, and engineering.

The Team Concept

Each of the teams in Plant F had a set of common character-istics. Each team had five to 25 members depending on the task to be performed. The teams each selected a team leader for coordi-nating responsibilities and interfacing with other areas. But each member of the team was to share responsibility for the performance of the total team and was expected to help meet the goals set by the team in conjunction with information provided by management. The team leaders reported to the supervisors, who maintained relationships with several teams. To as great an extent as possible, the teams were self-contained units sharing the following respon-sibilities with the management of the plant:

1. Meeting established production goals
2. Checking and maintaining established quality standards
3. Maintaining equipment and performing minor repairs
4. Training team members
5. Housekeeping
6. Coordinating with other teams
7. Providing feedback
8. Selecting a team leader
9. Maintaining safety programs
10. Keeping time for hours worked and balancing working hours

While engaging in teamwork, team members were expected to develop other responsibilities.

Listed below are the design teams' definitions of the various responsibilities as presented to hourly employees in the company employee handbook.[4]

1 MEETING ESTABLISHED PRODUCTION GOALS

The efficient production of batteries is a primary objective of Plant F and is vital to the plant's success.

Production goals, as established by support team personnel are based on studies of operator functions, manufacturing processes, equip-ment design and capability, etc., and information on such goals will be shared with team members.

All team members share in the responsibility for meeting the production goals of their team. As factors that affect production change, established production goals will undoubtedly change, and team members are expected to participate in the implementation of changes.

2 CHECKING AND MAINTAINING ESTABLISHED QUALITY STANDARDS

Maintaining the quality level of our product is the responsibility of every Plant F team member. The quality control responsibility, which we all share, is to maintain the desirability and salability of the product. Each of you perform tasks which affect other team members and our customers.

To maintain quality standards you must effectively identify quality problems through the use of testing, gauging, and audit programs. You must thoroughly understand your product and the equipment you use and follow up and coordinate corrective action when necessary.

The following questions regarding quality are important to you as a team member:

1) As I have performed my task will the product perform satisfactorily for the customer receiving it?
2) Are scrap, rejections, and reoperations at a minimum?
3) Are the manufacturing methods, handling, shipping, testing, under control to insure defect-free products?
4) Are our manufacturing methods compatible with our design?

Let's produce our product as if we were purchasing one ourselves.

3 MAINTENANCE AND MINOR REPAIRS

Plant F teams will be expected to perform maintenance and minor repairs on equipment and tooling used by their team. Team members will be expected to learn from one another and the maintenance service team to improve their ability in the maintenance area and keep their equipment in top working order at all times.

4 TRAINING TEAM MEMBERS

Training will be one of the primary functions of team members. Experienced team members will be expected to train new team members and current team members in the learning of new tasks.

5 HOUSEKEEPING

The cleanliness of our equipment, work place, and plant reflects upon the type of people we are and indicates the respect we have for each team member and for our company.

Each team will be responsible for its team area to see that it is kept clean during the shift and that it is clean at the end of the shift. Each team may determine the method they wish to use to accomplish the goal of "a place for everything and everything in its place."

Through effective housekeeping we can help illustrate to ourselves and to the community that we are successfully carrying out the concept of "People Helping People."

6 COORDINATING WITH OTHER TEAMS

The success of Plant F is dependent upon the efficient performance of all teams. Teams need to know how their everyday operations are affecting other teams in the plant. Coordinating with other teams in all areas of performance is a responsibility and a necessity.

7 FEEDBACK

"Feedback" is the primary path to understanding between individuals. It is essential to accomplishment, progress, and personal satisfaction. Two important requirements for effective "feedback" are that team members be willing to let the total Plant F team know what is on their minds and that the Plant team be willing to listen.

You as a team member need to be open and frank. You should expect and get the same treatment from any member of the Plant F team. Your "feedback" is important to the successful operation of our plant and to your satisfaction with your plant team. "Feedback" will also be given to you and your team from other Plant F teams.

8 SELECTION OF A TEAM LEADER

The operating teams will select their team leaders. During the selection process, each team must work within the philosophies and toward the goals of Plant F in conjunction with the Support Team.

9 MAINTAINING SAFETY PROGRAMS

Plant F is and will continue to be a safe place to work.

We are committed to providing and maintaining a safe working environment. It is the responsibility of each team member to share this commitment. "Working Safely" is an obligation to yourself, your family, your fellow team members, and the plant.

To implement safety, team members should:

1) Learn and respect all safety rules.
2) Follow all written and posted instructions.
3) Dress and groom themselves in a manner that is not disruptive to the plant operation.
4) Operate, maintain, and adjust equipment only after being properly instructed.
5) Feedback ways to improve safety.
6) Report all injuries to the medical department, regardless of how minor such injuries may appear.

10 KEEPING TIME FOR HOURS WORKED AND BALANCING WORKING HOURS

Each team member is responsible for accurately filling out a time card on a daily basis. Plant teams, under the direction and within the guidelines of the Support Team, will assume responsibility for balancing hours within their respective team.

SHARED RESPONSIBILITIES

The following responsibilities will be shared by team members, supervisors, and the Support Team.

1) Selecting new team members.
2) Meeting Equal Employment Opportunity requirements.
3) Making job assignments.
4) Assessing individual team member performance.
5) Counseling up to but not including discharge.
6) Movement from one team to another team.

1 SELECTING NEW TEAM MEMBERS

Each team shares with the Support Team in the selection of new plant team members.

2 MEETING EQUAL EMPLOYMENT OPPORTUNITY REQUIREMENTS

All teams and the Support Team have a responsibility to see that Equal Employment Opportunity requirements are met.

3 JOB ASSIGNMENTS

As a member of a plant team you will share with the Support Team in the assignment of jobs within your individual team.

4 ASSESSING INDIVIDUAL TEAM MEMBER PERFORMANCE

Working with members of the Support Team and your supervisors, team members will participate in determining the competency levels required for movement within and across teams.

5 COUNSELING PROGRAM

Since a cornerstone of the Plant F Employee Relations approach is mutual respect and trust, there is no need for a lengthy list of rules and regulations of conduct which carry with them a basic presumption of disrespect and mistrust.

There is only one rule — so self-evident as to not need advertising or posting on plant bulletin boards. It is simply this: "All employees respecting their own dignity, must respect the rights and privileges of their fellow employees, including the necessity of the entire business operation to achieve its fair and responsible objectives."

Any conduct by team members contrary to the above will result in counseling by your team leader, supervisor, or a member of the Support Team. If counseling is unsuccessful, or if conduct is in serious violation of our goals and philosophies, termination of employment will be necessary.

Our counseling program is a reflection of our slogan of "People Helping People" and our belief in respect for the individual. It is based on the principle that when a team member has a problem, he or she will be given the oppportunity to discuss this problem with any member of the Plant F Support Team.

6 MOVING FROM ONE TEAM TO ANOTHER

Team members who have learned all of the tasks on one team and who desire to move to another team should make such desire known to their fellow team members. At the start of each calendar quarter, 2 members of each team may move to a new team provided it is agreeable to both teams and the Support Team. Movement between teams must be consistent with the goals and philosophies of the plant, including Equal Employment Opportunity.

Hourly Pay System

Plant F adopted a combination seniority/skills-based pay system with five levels. At *Level 1* the new employee was expected to learn the basic operating responsibilities of a single job. *Level 2:* Mastery of a single job was demonstrated (no later than 90 days after hire). At this level employees were expected to learn the basic operating skills of the rest of the positions on a team. *Level 3:* After another six months of employment, or with demonstrated mastery of the rest of the positions on a team. At level 3 team members were expected to demonstrate capabilities in routine maintenance (i.e., setup, shutdown, fine-tuning) skills on all of the equipment in their area. *Level 4:* An employee begins the process of learning jobs on another team in a different operating area. *Level 5:* The employee would know all the basic operations in a second area. The system was intended to provide the opportunity for team members, if they so desired, to learn every operation in the plant within five years. It was believed the flexibility available with a workforce possessing multiple skills would prove invaluable to the success of the manufacturing operation.

Qualifications demonstrations for promotion were to be conducted by a team consisting of the production supervisor, a technical services supervisor, and team members.

Work Schedules

The plant operated normally on a five-day week with two eight-hour shifts. There was no regular rotation of work teams, and the supervisors stayed with their teams.

Desired Characteristics

At the conclusion of the design process, the seven key managers identified a number of characteristics they desired to have in their plant at the three-year point:

- Goals meaningful to all
- Shared trust, harmony, and friendship
- Cooperation and an orderly sense of direction
- Team commitment, with good communications and feedback
- Resources and results
- Opportunities and innovation
- Family involvement
- A highly profitable operation with customers requesting our product

- No turnover except that created by upward movement
- Community clamoring for more Federal Corporation operations
- Gained employee trust and loyalty
- Union kept out
- Initial workforce trained in (augmented) skills
- Record of low absenteeism and turnover
- Satisfied over government requirements
- Perfect safety record
- Good relationship among employee-community-plant
- In a position to actively go after new business
- Quality-conscious employees
- Well-maintained plant
- Local people advanced into positions of higher responsibility, with some of the original staff removed
- A proven track record of customer satisfaction
- Recognition as an innovative, successful operation

INTERNAL SOCIAL SYSTEM

Unless otherwise indicated we are discussing production supervisors in this section.

The Supervisor's Role

We have reviewed the fact that production supervisors were added to the plant at the insistence of the division management. They were not part of the original design, nor as we will see, did any detailed attention go into determining their role in the plant once they were hired. As the plant manager stated:

My boss said I had to have supervisors, so I hired supervisors. I was against the move but my hands were tied. I had my orders.

Supervisor Know-How

It should not be surprising that the level of technical expertise displayed by production supervisors was severely constrained by their lack of experience. At the time supervision was installed the plant support team made the conscious decision to trade for familiarity with operations under the Plant F style of management against technical and supervisory experience. A portion of this decision was forced on them by circumstances. Unable to attract transfers, they had to make internal promotions if they were to meet the divisional edict to install supervision.

Supervisors characterized their know-how in a variety of ways. Some could start up and shut down equipment but couldn't trouble-shoot. Some felt they could catch bit screw ups and spot bad parts. And others invested energy in learning the mechanics of the machinery by watching workers run the equipment.

As the plant evolved from start-up, there were two major areas of technical support for supervisors and their teams:

Technical Services. Consisting of a general supervisor and three supervisory positions, the technical services group provided the bulk of the major technical support to the organization:

> We do what is necessary to get people trained to run and sustain production.

Maintenance. Consisting of two area supervisors and 20 skilled trades trainees, the maintenance organization was intended to function in a traditional mode with additional emphasis placed on providing team members with skills for routine maintenance.

It is obvious that Plant F's overall low level of technical competence placed an enormous burden on the shoulders of the technical services and maintenance organizations to keep the plant running. Two technical service supervisors responded:

> Until recently we were incredibly overworked. We were the only people who were really acquainted with the equipment and we tried to fix everything ourselves. We realized a few months back that we couldn't continue this way. We needed to get people thinking for themselves and get some maintenance people trained up in order to lighten our load. For example, we've really put a lot of time into training up two mechanics to the point where the final assembly area can call on them first for repairs.

> Supervisors tend to want to rely on technical services to get their equipment running when it's down. They feel that calling us eliminates one of their problems and transfers the responsibility of getting machinery running to us.

The maintenance organization was faced with their own large developmental training needs. One maintenance supervisor remarked:

> There's very little industrial work in the area, so we've got some pretty inexperienced people working in the maintenance area. It's going to take quite a while before they can really carry their weight.

In order to keep the plant running, employees were encouraged to work to the utmost of their skills and capacities. Consequently, there were a lot of different hands with significantly differing degrees of expertise working on the equipment. This resulted in some major problems for maintenance and technical services at times. A maintenance supervisor reflected on the problem:

> The [team members] mean well but often do more damage than if they left the equipment alone. For a while, they used to tinker around and really screw up the equipment and then call us. Sometimes they still do.

Team members operated with a pay system that encouraged job movement within teams as well as movement to other teams. This resulted in employees not developing the expertise on single pieces of equipment that was more common in traditional operations. A technical services supervisor remarked:

> Job rotation is a real bear. Team members never seem to be able to pass along the technical expertise to the extent necessary for satisfactory performance in the job.

Supervisor Responsibility and Accountability

The team concept of operation at Plant F had a significant impact in assisting the process of diffusing responsibilities and pressures traditionally assumed to be the exclusive province of the supervisor role. Two area supervisors discussed this issue:

> The motto of this plant is "People Helping People" and that's really the way we do business around here. No one ever walks past someone else who's having problems without trying to help out.

> I want to see everyone concerned about production, cost, and unity and then I won't be needed. It's somewhat true right now.

Supervisors as a group appeared quite willing to push as much responsibility down as they felt people could handle. They remarked:

> I couldn't spread pressures down early on. Now I'm spreading all of it. The team understands it's their baby. If I get feedback that the job isn't getting done I shove it right back at them. Many people wanted to be told what to do when the pressure was on but I wouldn't do it.

> The management of this plant is quite lean and we need maximum output from each person, so I'll push down as much as the team can stand. They even schedule their own overtime, if necessary.

A few of the area supervisors relied heavily on the elected team leader to assist them in pushing down responsibilities:

> I'll call in the team leader, present the information, and ask, "What do we need to do. . . ?" to try to get him to feel the responsibility. I keep saying to the team, "This is your business — if we don't get these batteries out we'll lose X$."

A member of the support team provided some perspective on the development of this characteristic:

> When we hired them we didn't know what role the production supervisor would take. Some of them started out wanting to be the bossman; employees would follow his orders or they would be out. Given our earlier history this role didn't really fit and they got really frustrated. We had an O.D. consultant spend time with them to work through some of the ambiguity.

Supervisor Communications

Communications Management

Supervisors reported that their communications with the support team were quite good. The communication was characterized by informality, a limited amount of paper communications, and an emphasis on face-to-face communications. One supervisor remarked:

I feel really good about communications with the support team. It's not regularly scheduled and is quite casual. In performance appraisals (once a year) they are very honest with me — if I'm weak in some areas, they tell me about it. The only complaint I might have is that there is no follow-up on my development plans.

Supervisors felt relatively free to confront the support team with their concerns and suggestions and were generally quite positive about the reception they get:

The support team is always open for disagreement. It might not go my way but I can get it off my chest. I look at all of their suggestions and evaluate them and when possible let the team make their own adjustments if it will help them.

As long as the decision is not out of Division headquarters it's brought up for input. If you're convincing you'll get your way.

Communications with Team Members

Once again, area supervisors, as a group, felt quite positive about the quality of their communications with team members. A sample of supervisors remarked:

We're basically concerned about the people. What can we do in a particular department to make it more effective? I always go out and ask, "What's best for you?" And they're open with me.

I spend a great deal of time working through my team leaders and the communications flow is real good.

Teams held team meetings on approximately a once-a-week basis. Area supervisors did not necessarily participate in each of these meetings unless there was a specific agenda item calling for them to transmit information to the entire team or an issue that both the team and area supervisors agreed required their presence. As a result, the team meetings I observed were quite unstructured and appeared to serve a primary purpose of simply getting people together off the line. Aside from two small meeting areas, facilities for team meetings were generally nonexistent or inadequate.

Given the situation surrounding the introduction of supervisory personnel and their general lack of technical expertise, surprisingly few complaints of managerial interference were raised by the teams. One problem arose when a former production supervisor attempted to be extremely directive with the crews as he assumed his new position. He would make job assignments on a daily basis, for example, and the team members resented this. As a support team member put it:

> They would go to any support team member who would listen and complain. Attendance became poor and he suffered an increased number of personnel problems. We finally had to discharge him. When under pressure, he simply could not work from anything other than an authoritative model of supervision.

The goals of the original Plant F design called for a healthy questioning of policies and actions by all levels of the organization. An elaborate employee selection program/assessment center placed great weight in the hiring decision on employees' communications skills. These skills were very much evident in the day-to-day operation of the plant and, in the comment of one supervisor:

> If we make a decision that doesn't set right with the people, we'll all know about it in pretty short order. We must be able to explain most everything we do.

Supervisors recognized the importance of building strong interpersonal relationships with teams and team members indicated that listening skills were critical to this effort. My observations indicated considerably more supervisor-team member interaction at Plant F than at any other of the research sites. Supervisors bore that out with comments such as those below:

> I'm always making time to listen to people. If it's something really important we'll set up a time to talk off the line. If it's just a minor issue we'll discuss it immediately.

> I spend most of my day going around and talking to people. I'll bring up conversations and things on their mind will come out. Only 20 to 30 percent of it is directly work related.

Communication with Peers

For purposes of ease in presentation, this topic is addressed under four different categories: production supervisor/production supervisor; production supervisor/quality control supervisor; production supervisor/technical services and maintenance supervisors; and all supervisors as a group.

Production Supervisor/Production Supervisor. There appeared to be two general feelings about these relationships: what existed was good, and there was not enough of it. It appeared that communications between supervisors (outside of informal socializing) was often restricted to when a potential "border" dispute between operating areas surfaced.

Production Supervisor/Quality Control Supervisor. Two quality control supervisors were assigned the responsibility for covering the entire plant over a two-shift operation to support the production organization and monitor and troubleshoot quality problems. It appeared that their interface with manufacturing was quite positive. The quality control supervisors remarked:

> Problems with supervisors are rare and generally resolved face to face.

> Production Supervisors and I have to talk a lot — the people belong to him and the way he sees quality is generally the way the team sees it. I've had only 3 clashes in the last year and we've worked out compromises on each of them.

Production Supervisor/Technical Services and Maintenance Supervisors. The production supervisor-technical services-maintenance interfaces were often a source of frustration and/or dissatisfaction for all parties involved. The problems resided primarily in the low level of technical competence displayed by the individual production supervisors and the overworked situation technical services and maintenance supervisors found themselves in. The maintenance supervisors remarked:

> We'll argue over problems for a while and try to come to some conclusion; often we're simply left to finishing a job on the third shift.

> The biggest problem is that the production supervisors have no understanding of the time it really takes to fix a problem. They'll come into me sometimes and scream and yell a lot about this and that and they don't even know what they're talking about.

Technical services noticed some improvement in this area of concern in the few months before our visit:

> We're starting to get more of a breather. The production supervisor and/or maintenance can handle some of the more common problems and that frees up some of our time.

All supervisors as a group. The total supervisor group made great strides in improving communications within their group. In October 1977 they began a weekly meeting designed for information sharing and problem solving. Members of the support team could attend on an invitation basis only. One supervisor discussed the impact of the meeting:

> The supervisor meeting has been a big step in the right direction. Everyone is attending regularly and participation levels are high. The only problem we're really struggling with is our attempts at guessing what the support team wants us to do instead of determining what is best from our perspectives.

Supervisor Goal Setting and Motivating

Production goals were established by the support team in response to division requirements. The supervisor, and on occasion the superintendent, generally established departmental daily needs. The teams, however, had a great deal of flexibility around the work schedules they established for meeting the production requirements. (They did not, on the other hand, have flexibility around the production requirements.) For example, a team might schedule themselves to work two hours of overtime on a daily basis to avoid weekend work when production requirements were high.

The foundation of the Plant F operation – people helping people – was found in action in almost everything that took place in the plant. One supervisor remarked:

> My area has a new motivation, and that's the sign above them that says, "The world's best batteries start here," and we all really believe it.

Another stated:

We have four motivating factors:
1. We are here to make batteries.
2. We are here to meet production and quality needs.
3. We live by a handbook based on people helping people.
4. We're happy to be here.

We found little or no emphasis (beyond the catchwords and slogans above) on the part of supervisors to explicitly attempt to motivate their teams. Workers appeared to be highly self-motivated. Even the technical services and quality control supervisors (each of whom had no team members reporting to them) experienced little difficulty in getting team member support. A quality control supervisor remarked:

> We have no line people directly reporting to us but we have to get the best out of the team members. I will often identify "key" people in an area and lobby for their interest and support. It doesn't take much more than that to get things going.

The production supervisors as a group appeared to be equally as motivated. They routinely worked long hours and occasional weekends. Although the plant provided overtime compensation at the supervisory level it appeared that most supervisors generally did not list all the hours they worked for compensation purposes. One supervisor stated:

> If I stay over I'm generally learning something that will help me later on. I don't need to be paid for every minute I spend in the plant and I don't want to be either.

Supervisor as Trainer

Plant F provided for an intensive two-week training experience prior to employee hire. The Rapid Start program provided the prospective employee with a good working knowledge of the product, manufacturing processes, and the desired organizational culture. Once the employee began work, training was at best erratic in quality and timing and was relatively disorganized. One supervisor commented on how new workers were brought onboard:

Once an employee comes from Rapid Start, I turn him over to the team leader who brings him on board and gets him started learning his first job.

This informal training model, when combined with a lack of technical skills at the supervisor level, resulted in production supervisors spending very little of their time in direct on-the-job training or training evaluation activities, and the skills-based pay system suffering from a lack of consistent evaluation and promotion between areas. In some areas employees exercised key control over the evaluation and promotion process and have transformed the pay increases into little more than recognition for seniority.

Where supervisors did get involved in the training of team members, it was generally to inform and educate them on the use of new and different procedures. One supervisor commented:

We have a "red" book of procedures. I'll go over it with the team regularly and then put a team member in charge of keeping it up to date. The more training on procedures we provide employees with the better off we are.

There was recognition and concern among a number of technical services supervisors that the training issue was becoming an increasingly large problem:

The diffusion of the training process is critical to the success of this plant. Until we can get efficient transfer of learning we're going to run into problems, especially with the extent to which we have employees rotating jobs and areas.

Supervisor as Planner

Given the young age of the plant and the relative inexperience of the production supervisors it was not surprising to find that the bulk of the planning done by supervisors was of an extremely short-term day-to-day nature. As we observed supervisors in action, we were struck by the amount of time they spent in retracing prior steps and responding to immediate team and team member needs. There were, however, some characteristics of the plant's planning activities that were often resulting in problems. For example, employee rotation required supervisors to be constantly planning for the loss of experienced personnel and the integration of new inexperienced team members on a quarterly basis. This was consistently presented as a problem by a large majority of the Plant F personnel, yet there was little systematic planning evident to deal with the issue. Also, production scheduling was geared so closely to meeting immediate customer requirements that little effort was put into line balancing, developing optimal inventory levels, and so on. Consequently, the schedule changed with great regularity.

Given the ability of supervisors to fill up their workday and to be very busy simply by responding to immediate short-term needs, it became difficult to plan for a future role wherein supervisors would assume some of the existing support team responsibilities. There were a number of isolated incidents of supervisors taking on special projects, but it certainly was not the norm.

Much of what has been reviewed in this description of the supervisory role can be traced back to a telling statement made by a support team member:

> We've never really known what resources the teams need. That makes it difficult to plan around here.

Supervisor as Coordinator

At the plant's state of development at the time of our study, the supervisor played a major role in plantwide and interdepartmental coordination activities. Given the relative newness of the plant and the job rotation system, people generally were unable to develop the necessary expertise to move from mastering their individual jobs to moving on to assuming coordination responsibilities. The team leaders were beginning to assume some of these roles. One supervisor described the situation as follows:

> The teams look to me to schedule jobs and inform them of the tools they need and they want me to "run interference" for them. I'm beginning to get my team leader to handle some of the coordination needs.

In conceptualizing the supervisor's role in this area, the support team viewed a much lower profile for the area supervisor of the future:

The area supervisor of the future will spend much less time in coordination items. The team-to-team links that are developing will begin to exclude them.

ORGANIZATIONAL OUTCOMES: SUPERVISORY SATISFACTION AND EFFECTIVENESS

As a group the supervisors in Plant F were perceived generally as being effective in their roles. They ranked as the second most effective supervisory workforce in our sample of plants, ranking as being most effective (within our sample) in their interpersonal skills and their abilities to represent their groups' interest and reconcile it with others'. Not surprisingly, they ranked at the bottom of our sample in terms of their technical and professional skills.

Given our description of Plant F and the way in which the supervisory role was introduced, these findings are quite interesting. What appears to have happened is that supervisors were able to step in and fill a role in the plant not only without upsetting team members, but actually supporting them (at times almost in a go-fer role). And with everyone committed to making Plant F a success, any efforts directed at achieving that goal were appreciated and recognized. While, against any traditional description of a supervisor's role, the Plant F production supervisors appeared to have little to do, their role quickly established its usefulness to teams.

What is most encouraging are the levels of job satisfaction and the positive attitudes toward plant leadership indicated by the supervisors. Both measures were significantly higher than those of the second-ranking plant (Plant J) in our sample. Apparently supervisors did share the excitement and commitment of teams and team members, were grateful for the opportunity to fulfill this new higher-level role, and were continually appreciative of the opportunities the job presented to learn new skills.

FEEDBACK AND RENEWAL SYSTEMS

Communications among the people in the plant appeared to be generally good at all levels. The openness and trust that appeared to exist at Plant F served as an effective substitute for any formal means of generating data, solving problems, or introducing change.

The supervisors recognized the potential inadequacies of the informality and instituted regular information-sharing and problem-solving meetings. These sessions were looked at as a means of providing an effective renewal mechanism. There was an expressed intent on the part of the supervisors for that to be the case.

ANALYSIS OF THE SUPERVISORY SITUATION

We conclude our four case studies with a review of a supervisory workforce that is perceived as effective and that is satisfied. Yet little detailed attention was paid to the role, and it did not even exist in the minds of the management group at start-up. How can we begin to explain these outcomes?

Start-up Relationships

Key Tasks and Technologies. Plant F was designed for the production of a new model of maintenance-free automobile batteries, with a state-of-the-art and often untested technology.

Internal Social System. Management was committed to high degrees of employee participation and self-direction as a strategy to achieve high productivity and a satisfying work atmosphere.

Organizational Design. Management produced a general design that specified team responsibilities and shared responsibilities, relied on on-the-job training after introductory training, and called for no direct employee supervision. As part of the design process, the management clearly stated their goals and philosophy of operation and developed the slogan, "people helping people." A great deal of attention was directed at employee selection and orientation.

Individual Characteristics. The community provided little in the way of technically skilled, manufacturing oriented people. What it did provide were people who were attracted to the relatively high wages and security associated with a large employer, who exhibited communications skills during the assessment center that recommended their hire, and who became committed to the plant, its mode of operation, and its goals through a very effective orientation followed by a management that performed (as they promised) to employee expectations.

Organizational Outcomes. Initial production levels were quite disappointing. Everyone in the plant appeared to work up to maximum capacity in attempts to master the technology and get production on track. Outside technical resources were called in to help in the process.

Feedback and Renewal Systems. There appeared to be no formal mechanisms in place; however, the atmosphere of openness and trust that had developed fostered considerable two-way communications.

Shakedown

Supervisor-Organizational Design

The role of the production supervisor was an addition to the organizational design after approximately one year of less-than-satisfactory plant performance. People were selected for the job, were "thrown" out on the floor, and were basically left to find their way. The fact that employees were promoted from the hourly workforce appeared to be, retrospectively, a good choice. The supervisors assumed the position:

> My job is to help the teams to do theirs. I will do whatever I can to help them.

In fact, aside from one supervisor who was later dismissed, their initial role and mission appeared to them to be quite clear. Admittedly, ambiguities did appear over time, and corporate organizational development resources were called in to work with supervisors, but frustration and grumbling was at no time widespread.

As supervisors, they were still "people helping people."

Supervisor-Key Tasks and Technologies

The introduction of supervisors did little to improve a team's capacity to master the technology. Much of that credit belongs to the outside resources and technical services and maintenance supervisors who patiently worked with team members.

Supervisors were generally technically deficient and spent little time directly troubleshooting or problem-solving around equipment. This placed a continuing burden on the existing technical resources at the plant.

Supervisor-Internal Social System

The supervisors appeared to carve out roles that largely were defined by the teams. To some teams they were "father confessors" available whenever a team member wanted someone to talk to, for some they were message carriers and/or go-fers, for other teams they were an additional hired hand.

Generally, there appeared to be minimal status distinction between supervisors and their work teams. Supervisors generally conformed to the existing norms of teams and were found to be useful to have around. With this situation it is not surprising that we found few cries of "management interference" by team members.

As long as the plant ran well, the support team would not direct a great deal of attention to the production supervisors. And when production was less than satisfactory, supervisors were not blamed. In fact there was extremely little blaming or finger pointing evident throughout the organization.

Key Tasks and Technologies-Organizational Design

In the absence of detailed knowledge of how to operate the new technology, the organizational design had to be deliberately vague regarding job descriptions. However, the listing of team responsibilities (both sole and shared) was comprehensive in its coverage of the key organizational tasks.

One apparent problem in this area was related to the pay system which, although encouraging fairly rapid rotation, discouraged workers from gaining any real expertise on individual pieces of equipment.

Key Tasks and Technologies-Internal Social System

The significant skill gaps that existed in the organization (and most specifically in the teams) were a major factor in the poor start-up. At the same time, the teams demonstrated such high levels of commitment to the plant's success that the short term assignment of outside resources led to a rapid and dramatic improvement in the work team's capacity to operate the plant successfully.

Organizational Design-Internal Social System

The intents of the design team appeared to have generally become a reality. The principles underlying the Plant F design were widely shared and ascribed to. The practice people helping people could be found throughout the plant. As we mentioned earlier, the lack of explicit design attention to the supervisor's role appeared to create few, if any, problems in the plant.

SUMMARY

Federal Products Corporation's Plant F created a highly partici-pative work culture built around the slogan, "people helping people." Behaviors directed at meeting the requirements of the operating slogan, and the strong commitment of the workforce, appeared to have offset many of the possible negative effects of the lack of explicit structure in the supervisor's role.

Plant F's notions of worker self-direction were broad in scope. Outside of production goal setting, workers were involved in virtually all decisions affecting their work and in a sizable number of plant-wide decisions. They were heavily involved in scheduling of overtime and weekend work and were knowledgeable in the basic economics of battery manufacturing and plant operations.

As we mentioned earlier in the section, supervisors were added to the plant as a "lay-on" from division management. One must conclude that the addition of supervisors did not have any significant negative impacts on the system and did, in fact, have a number of positive impacts highlighted earlier. Team members accepted the legitimacy of their presence and learned to mutually carve out roles for each other. The supervisors developed into true resource persons, assisting the teams in whatever areas seemed necessary from working on the floor, to tracking down spare parts, to interfacing with other areas, and so on.

The fact that the production supervisors were promoted from the hourly workforce helps explain much of the success in role defi-nition we observed. All supervisors were highly appreciative of the confidence expressed in their abilities by their promotions. They were thoroughly versed in the plant culture at start-up and were committed to keeping the high levels of participation and positive spirit.

Most supervisors expressed little concern over the future of their role in the plant and had great trust and confidence in the ability of the support team and the divisional management to absorb them into other positions should the situation arise where that became a necessity. The general feelings of the supervisors could be summarized by the following statement:

> I don't worry much about my future role. I've got so much to learn
> in my current position and I know when the time comes, the support
> team will take care of me.

In our experience with other plants over the years we have never seen such a strong, healthy, and lasting culture built on the foundation of a simple slogan. The plant's operations identified quite closely with ideologically based communities with one significant difference; the plant's profit-making orientation. It will be quite useful to revisit this plant after a number of years to continue our examination.

In short, Plant F addressed the question of supervisory roles and responsibilities by letting it evolve over time with little coordinated direction from above. They selected a supervisory force of formerly hourly employees who were extremely grateful for the opportunity to assume a nonexempt position regardless of the duties of the position. And they minimized the direct accountability of supervisors for hard-number results, preferring instead to keep responsibility vested in the team.

NOTES

1. Internal documents, 1974.
2. Company employee handbook, 1975.
3. Company employee handbook, 1975.
4. Company employee handbook, 1975.

7

Implications for Action and Research

In this brief concluding chapter we shall step back from our case studies and explore the implications of our conceptual framework for managers, supervisors, behavioral science practitioners, and researchers. Earlier it was stated that the ultimate validity of this effort lies in the ability to assist these groups in their efforts to design and manage the supervisory role in a manner that will ensure high levels of satisfaction and effectiveness with the occupants of these roles. What follows is the conclusion of our attempt at providing that assistance.

ACTION IMPLICATIONS

Plant Start-up

Chapter 2 outlined the ways in which each of the elements of the model influenced the organizational outcomes and were in turn influenced by the outcomes, through the feedback and renewal systems.

In order to understand and predict supervisory satisfaction and effectiveness in a start-up situation, one needs to gather information on the initial states of the elements in the framework and recognize the kinds of impacts that the elements can have on outcomes, and vice versa. When considering the situation faced by the designers of organizations in addressing the supervisory role, it is appropriate to ask the following questions: What is the anticipated state of each of the elements as they have been designed? What, if anything, can change in the design of these elements or might change shortly after start-up? How would each of these changes affect supervisory satisfaction and effectiveness?

The implications of engaging in a questioning process such as the one outlined above are clear: Designers need to invest significant energy in analyzing the supervisory role in advance of the plant start-up. Plant F's failure to address this question at their start-up contributed to enormous start-up problems due to the insufficient presence of experienced resources. Plant G's dramatic overestimation of team member capacities at start-up and their abilities to master the technology contributed to similar problems. Only at Plants J and O did we see any significant attention paid to the unique demands of the supervisory role in their organizations. The extent to which they acted on their conclusions, contributed, in large part in our opinion, to the greater success of their start-ups.

We are not saying that problems surrounding the supervisory role at start-up cannot be remedied over time. We are simply arguing that it is much easier to produce a sound and comprehensive plant design that includes consideration of the supervisory role (and allows for evolution and adaptation) prior to start-up, than after the plant is in operation. While Plant F ultimately was quite successful, we would argue that front-end recognition of this issue could have expedited the process by which they achieved their success.

Shakedown

We have highlighted the importance, over the moderate to long run, of providing a total organizational design in which each of the elements fits or is congruent with each other. Many of the issues perceived as supervisory problems in the sites studied are an outgrowth of misfits, the most pervasive of which were described in the research sample.

We emphasized the need for managers to engage in a continuing plant diagnosis that continually assesses the following questions: Are any of the relationships among the elements in a state of misfit? What types of changes appear to have created these misfits? What actions can we take to bring the relationship(s) back into a state of congruence? Will these actions stimulate any further misfits?

Obviously, such activity requires that the management of a plant be constantly in touch with the pulse of the operation. It implies that the continuing evaluation and fine-tuning of the organization be identified as a high-priority item, as in the case of Plant J.

We have observed a tendency on the part of managers to become wedded to a particular design element or feature and to be unwilling to address its appropriateness in the face of overwhelming negative evidence. Plant G provided a clear example of such a problem with its unwillingness to address questions of supervisor-team relationships unless faced with overwhelming supervisor discontent and with its insistence on not outlining the supervisory role in writing in the face of apparently irreconcilable role ambiguity. Managers must be flexible and recognize the need to not become "too" committed to a design.

What are some potential action items for managers during shakedown periods? We will review the misfits highlighted in Chapter 2 and discuss some action implications that grow out of our framework.

Neglect of Start-up vs. Shakedown vs. Relative Maturity Distinctions

The avoidance of major problems in this area requires a detailed understanding at start-up, and continuing attention to, the production task and technology and its implications for task complexity, necessary operating skills, and the amount of time and talent required to learn them.

As outlined earlier, Plants G and F provided clear examples of organizations that had dramatically underestimated the demands of a start-up and had encountered significant problems as a result.

At the other extreme, Plant J produced a comprehensive design for a limited start-up that provided mechanisms for legitimizing organizational changes as it grew and matured. Although Plant J developed a document describing the characteristics of the ideal supervisor, management recognized that they would never have people with these qualities and shells without making a significant training investment. Their most significant failure lay in their inability to predict the adjustment problems that would be experienced by business managers and directors at start-up and their consequent impact on supervisors attempting to figure out their place in the organization.

Unrealistic Assumptions Regarding Work Group Developmental Trends

Work teams within a single plant develop at different rates and can plateau at different levels of self-direction capacity for a variety of reasons. Often, managers have not explicitly accepted or tolerated this diversity and have therefore not managed it well.

If one recognizes this diversity, the implications are clear. It is probably not appropriate to think of completely eliminating the role of first line supervision over time, and, in fact, one should plan for contingencies requiring an increase as well as a decrease in the supervisory presence over time. Designers and supervisors should also recognize and legitimize diversity among work teams in terms of the amount of responsibility and autonomy delegated to them at any point in time.

Plant G again provides the clearest examples of problems in this area. We observed the tendency of work teams in this plant assuming a relationship that mirrored their supervisors. Those working with a technically competent supervisor exhibited the best productivity levels yet exhibited little self-direction capacity. Other teams exhibited a great deal of self-direction capacity yet performed poorly. There was little recognition of the role the supervisors played in these very different teams.

In Plant F, the plant providing for the least supervisory presence, problems occurred when people transferred from team to team. The system was designed in such a way that the most experienced team members would be the ones to transfer and provided no mechanism for replacing the loss. If it was a single person, the supervisor would pitch in and assist the team until it developed sufficient mastery to replace the loss. However, often the loss involved more than one person, and the accommodations were more difficult to make.

Plant O was quite clear on the issue of supervisory presence. When the team had problems that would significantly affect results the supervisor was expected to be involved with (or at least informed of) problem resolution activities. The supervisory profile could vary from team to team and within a single team on an almost daily basis. Whereas their way of handling the issue did stifle employee self-direction over the long term, they experienced none of the problems we saw in Plant G, for example.

The model presented in Chapter 3 highlighted the need to recognize that the supervisory role changes as workers and work groups achieve different levels of self-direction capacity. Aside from Plant O, none of the plants provided training to supervisors that allowed them to assume new roles vis-a-vis the team. Consequently, except for Plant F, where the teams played the major role in deciding what supervisors would do, and for Plant O, which we have just reviewed, significant problems were encountered.

Insufficient System Stability

Managers must take care to avoid the unnecessary disruption of an organization that by nature of its participative, worker self-directing orientation is already constantly changing. While it is critically important to have a clear philosophical understanding of team development and delegation of responsibilities by supervisors over time, it is equally important to recognize that these are processes that are taking place among individuals who must know, respect, and trust each other.

Plants O and G provided us with classic examples of problems in this area. At Plant O, college educated supervisors directed their efforts, with almost single-minded dedication, to doing a good enough job to get offshifts. Little attention was paid to the implications of introducing new supervisors (every two or three years) at various stages of work group development. At Plant G, supervisors were rotating shifts on a six-month basis while teams stayed on single shifts. Six months was scarcely enough time to build a solid, trusting relationship with a work group.

Although Plant F never engaged in a process of supervisory role definition over time, it was able, for a variety of reasons explored in Chapter 6, to build strong trust relationships between supervisors and work groups. The strength and quality of these relationships, when combined with the employee population's commitment to people helping people and the plant's success, served over the moderate run to overcome a lot of the obvious misfits that were an outgrowth of inadequate planning. Over the long run, the plant, again without any formal planning (and apparently without articulating it) evolved into a satisfactory and sound structure and operating system given the state of the other elements.

Underestimating in Supervisory Recruitment and Selection

Supervisory selection is not a matter to be left to chance after a design is complete. It must be addressed in concert with a thorough analysis of the key tasks and technologies; the individual characteristics of workers, managers, and existing supervisors; the philosophical and practical goals of employee self-direction; and the availability of career paths beyond the supervisory level (lateral and upward).

Here, none of the four plants escaped significant problems. In Plant O, the problems were between college and upgrade supervisors, in Plant G between technical and nontechnical supervisors, in Plant J with their seeming inability to recruit outsiders successfully, and in Plant F, with its original intention to have no manufacturing supervisors at all. The problems at Plants G and F could be traced to inadequate planning. Plants O and J had problems stemming from a more complex source. Plant O's problems tied to an inadequate understanding of the impact of various elements in the supervisory career development program on role occupants. Plant J's problems were related to an inability or unwillingness to establish a successful recruiting program.

While attention to the four elements outlined above is quite time consuming, it can head off many of the problems reviewed in this study.

Underresourcing Supervisory Skill Development

In time, managers and supervisors must be able to identify and develop a list of skills necessary for them to make their desired contribution to the plant. Also, adequate training resources — both formal and informal — must be allocated to assist supervisors in obtaining these skills.

Aside from Plant O, and to a lesser extent Plant J, none of the plants in our study was successful in this activity. All experienced problems. In Plant G, supervisors were often unable to facilitate team development because of their own lack of skills. In Plant F, supervisors were often having to run to technical services to solve problems brought to them by team members.

At Plant J, the problems were less significant but nonetheless worthy of mention. Supervisors often acted in a vacuum of performance feedback and were forced to choose and develop their own priorities. These priorities did not necessarily reflect those of their superiors.

Supervisory Evaluation and Reward Systems
Not Tied to Team Development

It is appropriate for managers to work with supervisors to establish timetables for their responsibilities as a developer of a work group, and it is also appropriate to establish benchmarks for determining to what level a group's capabilities have been developed. This strategic aspect of the supervisory role in participative work systems is clearly amenable to some form of goal setting, systematic assessment, and reward. It tends not to be treated in this way.

Only at Plant O did such activities take place with regularity. Unfortunately, the evaluation systems were so cumbersome and time consuming they were viewed as an additional burden for already overworked supervisors.

Plant J also developed an apparently cumbersome and time consuming system that met with great resistance by managers who felt they had too many time demands to conduct evaluation sessions.

It is a bit incongruous that so much attention, at three of our plants, went into the design of a skills-based reward system for workers, and little attention was paid to the evaluation and reward systems for supervisors.

Absence of Supervisory Support Systems

The remedy for this problem is relatively straightforward, once the need is recognized: Anticipate the need to build relationships among supervisors and take steps to legitimize concern about their productivity and the quality of their work life.

Relative Maturity

We must focus our attention on the plant's long-range ability to remain flexible and to adapt to the inevitable changes it will face.

This ability is related, in large part to the state of its elements and to the extent to which they inhibit or promote flexibility.

In addition, over time, one or more elements emerge as key factors — elements that determine the direction in which the plant evolves. It is especially important that these key factors not inhibit flexibility.

In addressing long-range issues surrounding the supervisory role, one must attempt to answer the following questions:

Does the plant have any key factors? If so, what are they? Why?

How has that key factor been changing over time? In what direction is it moving? What are the implications for the supervisory role if other elements are changed to avoid misfits?

To what extent do the elements inhibit or promote flexibility?

Is the plant investing resources to increase the flexibility promoting capacity of the elements?

SUMMARY

There are no easy solutions to the question of designing supervisory roles in participative work systems in a way that is both satisfying and effective. The most significant lesson of this research is that the role of the supervisor cannot be studied apart from the total organization. It should be an integral part of any design process and requires continuing attention as a plant and its workforce develop over time.

IMPLICATIONS FOR RESEARCH

The nature of this research is exploratory. At the time of the study there was little or no published information on the supervisory role under conditions of relatively high employee participation. And the supervisory role, under any plant conditions, has been greatly ignored for the past 15 to 20 years.

This research calls for a reawakening among researchers of the critical role of employee supervision in organizations, as well as for the recognition that the supervisor does play a role worthy of examination.

In addition, we still have much to learn about the dynamics of employee participation in different kinds of organizations. The only way to accomplish much of this task is through continued insightful clinical observation. It is my hope that this research spawns just such a program of continued clinical research.

Existing theoretical conceptions of leader-follower relationships need to be reformulated to encompass the shared responsibility and authority relationships documented in this study. Frameworks of group-centered leadership are going to become increasingly important for practitioners as quality of work life activities increase in the United States.

Appendix: Research Procedures and Methodology

The management literature provides little other than the identification of the supervisory role under conditions of relatively high employee participation as a problem warranting research attention. Our current state of knowledge indicated it would be premature to attempt to develop hypotheses for rigorous testing.

Furthermore, we were of the opinion that a hypothesis testing research design would provide little in the way of helpful data for those taking action in addressing the supervisory role. With organizational systems of great complexity and a highly dynamic supervisory role, a limited set of hypotheses and variables for examination could not adequately describe the phenomena under review.

Therefore, a two-phase exploratory study was adopted with two principal objectives in mind. Our first objective was to describe, through a number of analytical case studies at selected sites, the types of supervisory roles and functions uniquely or especially associated with increased levels of employee participation and the consequences of this modified role for individual satisfaction and individual and organizational performance. The second objective was to iteratively develop and refine, on the basis of the case studies and questionnaire results, a conceptual framework that will assist us in understanding the supervisory role in participative organizations. The development of such a framework serves as a necessary prerequisite for more systematic and quantitative research.

The research has been validated in a number of ways.

Accuracy of Factual Data. Factual information provided has been cross-checked in interviews with the different people at each research site and, where appropriate and available, through examination of internal company documents and observation of manager-supervisor-worker and work group interaction on the floor during working hours.

Validity of Analysis on a Plant-by-Plant Basis. At the conclusion of our research at the individual plants, preliminary case studies were written and forwarded to the research sites for review. These case studies, which presented the data collected and analyzed the supervisory role in the context of our preliminary conceptual framework, were reviewed by plant management and supervisors. Our analyses and conclusions were subjected to critique and were modified accordingly.

Testing of Conceptual Framework. Our conceptual framework has been tested in a number of ways. Initially, it was tested for its internal logic, consistency, and comprehensiveness. Second, it was tested for its power as an explanatory vehicle for our findings of supervisory satisfaction and effectiveness and for the individual, interpersonal, and group dynamics in the four cases.

The ultimate validity of our research lies in its ability to assist managers in designing and managing the supervisory role in a way that results in high levels of supervisory satisfaction. In recent months, I have engaged in the beginning of just such a validation process through consultation with a number of sites in this study.

Kurt Lewin once stated, "There is nothing as practical as a good theory." With experience, we will know of the practicality of our work.

DEVELOPMENT OF THE CONCEPTUAL FRAMEWORK

Our field exploration was not conducted tabula rasa — without prior notions of the phenomena under review. The data collection and interpretation of results were guided by a simple preliminary model of the supervisory role in the face of increasing levels of worker and work group participation. This model evolved from a pilot site study, interviews with consultants involved in quality of work life projects, and personal understanding of the problem rooted in my prior experience with the problem as a practicing manager.

In this model the supervisory role was viewed as being affected by three major factors: (1) individual characteristics of the supervisory workforce; (2) supervisory work situation; and (3) technical, social, administrative capacities and capabilities of the hourly workforce. The individual characteristics category includes demographic, cultural, educational, and managerial descriptors comprising the supervisory workforce. The supervisory work situation refers to the organizational design characteristics that influence the supervisory role (i.e., employee participation philosophy and strategy, employee recruitment and selection, pay and promotion systems, technology, spans of control). The last category refers to the existing state of development of the hourly workforce against an assessment of their potential capacity to assume additional responsibilities. An illustration of the model is presented in Figure A.1.

FIGURE A.1
Preliminary Model of the Supervisory Role in Participative Work Systems

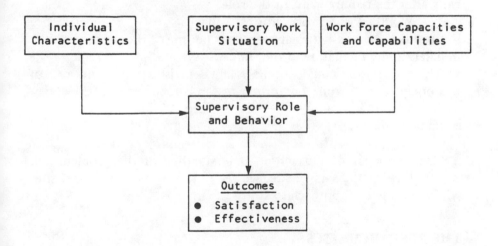

FOCUSING THE RESEARCH EFFORT

The specific focus of the research effort was on studying the supervisory role in organizations that had endeavored to significantly increase the level of employee participation in day-to-day and/or plant affairs. We restricted our focus to only such organizations, rather than a broader sample that would include more traditional plants, because the available literature on supervision in traditional plants appeared to provide an adequate basis for comparison.

Our initial efforts were composed of detailed interviews with a broad sample of managers, supervisors, and workers at a single plant site. The purpose of this activity was to assess the interest of potential organizational sponsors in the planned research, to determine the feasibility of the simple model as a guide for our research efforts, and to provide data useful in organizing the total research project. These interviews provided us with three key caveats that guided our further study.

1. The supervisory role in participative work systems was highly dynamic; a number of factors maintained the potential to dramatically alter the requirements of the role.
2. Workers' and work groups' capacities to exercise influence in organizational activities appeared to be one of the major variables in determining the nature of the supervisory role.
3. Supervisors could not be studied in isolation of the rest of the organization. While our prime research focus was on the supervisory role, the total management system of the plant had to be examined.

On the basis of our initial understanding of the problem and our findings at the sample site, we set out to secure additional sites while refining our approach to study them.

THE RESEARCH SITES

We began our search for research sites by developing a list of a dozen organizations reputed to operate with high levels of employee participation. Each of these organizations was contacted by letter or by phone with a follow-up letter. Depending upon the organization contacted, initial communication took place with the corporate manager of organization development, a plant manager of organization development, or a plant manager. One-day site visits were arranged with eight of the organizations that expressed a preliminary interest in the research project. These visits were intended to provide us with the opportunity to assess the organization as a possible research site and allowed the organization (as represented by management and supervisors and generally a sample of workers) to understand the commitments entailed in their participation in the project and determine the extent of their interest in involvement. All the sites agreed to participate in the study after the site visits. We dropped one site, determined as an unsuitable research site (i.e., the management of the organization dramatically overstated the level of employee participation), and were left with seven sites. At each of the seven plants included in the final sample we had the cooperation of all levels of the hierarchy. In addition, each plant had identified the supervisory role as a problem warranting examination and/or remedial action. Plant management characterized the problem in a number of different ways:

> Our supervisors are really in a bind and are really upset over their role in the plant.

> Our supervisors are unable to cope with the demands of our operations and we don't quite understand why.

> We have more problems with our supervisors here than at any other plant I've ever worked in.

> Our supervisors are beginning to get edgy about their future in the plant.

The sample of seven plants represented various industries utilizing technologies of differing complexity. There was significant variation in plant size and age. And while they all were committed to significantly more participation than is the norm in U.S. industrial plants, they nevertheless presented a relatively broad continuum of desired worker participation as determined by study of available plant mission statements, operating philosophies and other relevant documents. The sites are described in Table A.1.

TABLE A.1
Research Sites

Extent of Desired Worker Participation*	Site Name	Industry	Size	Age of Site
Rather limited	L	Sheet metal	25	20
	C	Disposable diapers	1,650	10
	O	Consumer paper products	900	5
	G	Ball bearings	400	3
	B	Wiring harnesses	320	1
Relative	J	Diesel Engines and components	470	3
self-direction	F	Automotive batteries	350	3

*The continuum identified in this category is an outgrowth of a review of published information made available to the researcher and discussions with managers and supervisors during preliminary site visits. The order listed here was later confirmed by the data collected in the field and through the questionnaires.

Thus our sample of sites provided us with a significant variety of situations and wide range of technological complexity, size, age, and so forth.

Before scheduling the plant for an in-depth site visit, we conducted a thorough review of available documents in order to enhance our understanding of the nature of the organization and its development. Organizational design manuals, statements of organization purpose, past diagnostic reviews, organization charts, and production histories proved important in directing our questions during our on-site research.

ON-SITE RESEARCH: INTERVIEWS

The on-site plant visits represented our major clinical efforts to understand and describe the phenomena under study. In this phase, lasting a full week at each plant, we interviewed those individuals most directly involved in defining the nature of the supervisory role. These interviews were held on each of the four levels described in Figure A.2.

Our interviews began with a representative sample of plant management at level 2, followed by interviews with supervisors at level 3. A small sample of workers (10 to 15 at each site) at level 4

FIGURE A.2

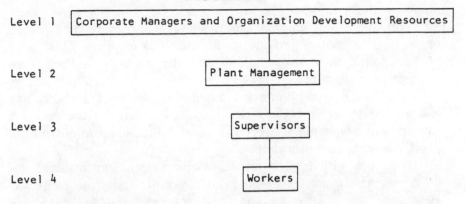

Level 1 | Corporate Managers and Organization Development Resources

Level 2 | Plant Management

Level 3 | Supervisors

Level 4 | Workers

was also interviewed, in considerably less depth than those conducted at levels 2 and 3. Our final set of interviews was held with corporate managers and organization development resources at level 1.

In our interviews with level 2, our research questions moved from a general concern for management's intentions to develop a participative organization and their subsequent design or redesign activities to specific questions regarding the supervisors' role in the organization and their assessment of performance and problems to date. Interviews with top management at level 2 included the following questions: Why have you increased the traditional levels of employee participation in this organization? How did you go about establishing your organization design? What attention was paid to the supervisory role in the design process? What is your assessment of the supervisory role in this plant today and in the future? How does it differ from your perceptions of the traditional supervisory role?

Interviews with middle managers at level 2 focused heavily on their roles as supervisors of supervisors. Questions included the following: What is your assessment of the supervisory role in this plant today and in the future? How do you view your role as supervisor of supervisors? What are the strengths and weaknesses of this plant's participative mode of operation? What distinguishes success ful from unsuccessful supervisors in the plant?

The interviews conducted with supervisors at level 3 were conducted in great depth (45 minutes to 2 hours) and focused on the following key areas: their backgrounds, their views on the plant's participative mode of operation, their definition of the supervisory role — how it has (or has not) changed over time, and their satisfaction with the role.

A great deal of emphasis in the level 3 interviews was placed on having supervisors provide us with critical incidents illustrative of the points they were making and the phenomena they were attempting to describe.

In informal level 4 interviews with a sample of workers, we endeavored to explore their views on their role(s) in the research site operating system, the supervisory and management roles, and the plant's development over time.

Interviews with level 1 corporate management and organization development resources focused primarily on the way the plant was viewed in the context of the total company and the corporate assessment of problem issues facing the plant. These interviews were also used to gain information on the plant's efficiency and effectiveness in the context of corporate expectations and other plant results.

Altogether 208 interviews were conducted during the on-site phase of the research project. Notes were taken in each of the interviews and later organized on a topical basis.

Table A.2 summarizes the distribution of these interviews across each of the sites at different levels.

TABLE A.2
Distribution of Interviews by Plant and Level

Plant	Level 1	2	3	4	Total
L	2	4	4	8	18
C	3	8	12	10	33
O	3	9	13	12	37
G	1	8	13	6	28
B	2	6	11	8	27
J	2	8	12	15	37
F	2	6	8	12	28
Total	15	49	73	71	208

SYSTEMATIC OBSERVATION

Upon concluding the in-depth interviews with level 3 supervisors, we spent one to two days "shadowing" supervisors as they went through their daily work routine. The direct observation of actual supervisory behavior proved invaluable in gaining an appreciation of the supervisory role not possible with basic interviewing. Where observational data differed significantly from the data collected in interviews, we pursued the deviations in an effort to understand their sources and further strengthen the credibility of our clinical findings.

CLINICAL DATA PROCESSING AND ANALYSIS

During the field work portion of the research project, organized research notes were written up upon completion of each of the research sites. These notes contained our impressions and observations of the site along with the diagnostic report fed back to the site sponsors. The organization of our research findings was strongly guided by our preliminary model (Fig. A.1).

The preliminary model underwent refinement and elaboration with each successive plant visit, as we uncovered an increasing number of variables and relationships that appeared to influence significantly the supervisory role. After completing all the site visitations, we were able to develop a more refined model of the supervisory role described in Chapter 2. We returned to our data and tested this model against each of the plant sites to ensure its comprehensiveness and validity.

To avoid overloading readers with extensive case studies of each of the plants, we chose to document only four research sites (Plants O, G, J, and F) in this study. It is our belief that the four sites chosen for presentation provided the researcher and consequently, the reader, with a comprehensive overview of the data available from the total sample and warranted not including the other case studies.

Index

About the Author

Leonard Schlesinger is currently assistant professor of business administration at the Harvard Business School, where his teaching and research is in organizational behavior and human resource management. He received his bachelor's degree from Brown University, an MBA in corporate and labor relations from Columbia University and a doctorate in organizational behavior from the Harvard Business School. Before joining the Harvard faculty in 1978 he served in a number of manufacturing, industrial relations and organizational development positions with Procter and Gamble and held the position of Associate Coordinator of Youth Services in the State of Rhode Island.

The bulk of Professor Schlesinger's recent research has focused on (1) organizational innovations designed to foster employee productivity and quality of work life and (2) the strategic readaptation of organizations in response to changes in technology, markets, regulation, and/or workforce demographics. He is author of five books and several articles in scholarly and management oriented journals.

Professor Schlesinger is a member of the Academy of Management and a member of the board of the Organizational Behavior Teaching Society. He also serves as a member of the editorial boards of *Exchange* and the *Academy of Management Review*.

As a management consultant, Professor Schlesinger has worked with a wide variety of organizations in the United States, Canada, and Mexico. He lives in Arlington, Massachusetts, with his wife Phyllis, a specialist in managerial career development, and their two daughters.